PRAISE FOR *DANCE WE DO*

"Through Ntozake Shange's personal memories of dance—what it has meant to her, how she came to know, understand, and feel it—we are taken on a journey that chronicles some of the greatest dancers and choreographers of the latter part of the twentieth century."

—PHYLICIA RASHAD

"Ntozake Shange's *Dance We Do* is a gorgeous last offering from one of our most gifted and multifaceted artists. Her passion for dance, just like her passion for words, is among the many reasons she will be missed, though these insightful interviews, ruminations, and reflections will continue to be a balm, across generations, from her to us."

—EDWIDGE DANTICAT,
author of *Everything Inside*

"A workaholic to her last breath, Ntozake Shange has left us with a book that expands our knowledge of Black dance. Not only is it a textbook, but it was composed by someone who created a new form. A true innovator."

—ISHMAEL REED,
author of *Malcolm and Me*

"In *Dance We Do*, Ntozake Shange presents a language of movement that only she knew—relearned with clarity and courage, and unveiled to the world as a black American groove of words in commemorative motion."

—REBECCA CARROLL,
author of *Sugar in the Raw: Voices of
Young Black Girls in America* and host of the
podcast *Come Through with Rebecca Carroll*

"As a dancer and a writer and a Black girl in a Black body with Black dreams and Black fears and Black hopes and no idea how to shape the world or the words, Ntozake Shange was my teacher and my mother. The magic and the magician. She was the blueprint. She was the road map. She was the beacon; the light. Dance was my first language, the way I learned to speak before I knew the written word would be my weapon of choice. *Dance We Do* is a praise song for dance and dancers. It is a love poem for anyone who has ever looked in wonder as a dancer defies gravity with their body and casts spells with their presence.

Ntozake Shange delivered her gifts to us embossed with directions, and permission, to create our own magic and miracle and movement. *Dance We Do* is her final gift to us, but it is, like she was, a gift that will nourish and replenish us for generations to come.

In her most noted works, Shange taught us how to sing a Black girl's song; in *Dance We Do*, she teaches us how important it is to move with it too."

—BASSEY IKPI,
author of *I'm Telling the Truth, but I'm Lying*

"In *Dance We Do*, Ntozake Shange offers the living history of Black dance our current movements need. In these conversations' exquisite choreography, we witness the artist's incomparable poetic stretch, her dazzling theoretical reach, and her unparalleled ability to name the deep political necessity of Black bodily knowledge. Here, we see Shange as teacher and theorist, charting the spiral histories of Black dance with the eloquence of a lyrical rond de jambe. Her keen and tender reflections on dance greats such as Dianne McIntyre and Dyane Harvey set the beat for interviews with newer voices like Camille A. Brown and Davalois Fearon, alongside whom we learn from Shange's great vision and pedagogy. To read

Dance We Do is to move with a master. It is to learn not only what Black dance means, why Black bodies matter, but *how*. *Dance We Do* makes its meanings elegantly, fearlessly, with the endless precision of Blackness itself: a full vocabulary of bodies and lives, writing rhythms that out-move time."

—MECCA JAMILAH SULLIVAN, PHD,
author of *Blue Talk and Love*

"Blessed are we to have a new work by the inimitable Ntozake Shange, whose writing is a balm for the soul. Sharing with readers her earliest body memories, Shange takes us into the most intimate spaces of her own fleshy form and, by extension, those of the oft overlooked Black dancers she spotlights. She makes us feel the connections between body and brain, the ache of overworked muscles, the discipline required to make jetés and fouettés appear effortless, as we linger on every word of this taut work of Black brilliance, wanting our eyes to forever dance on its pages."

—TANISHA C. FORD,
author of *Dressed in Dreams: A Black Girl's
Love Letter to the Power of Fashion*

"*Dance We Do* holds an eternal flame for the embodied work and life of Ntozake Shange. This new work is our spiritual relevé. It helps us rise to our toes and once again honor Black bodies as beautiful, magical, and elegant. Each chapter is a radical intervention that brings us closer to the Black Radical Tradition of exploring our rhythms. Shange has always known that Black Lives Matter, and this text is a reminder of her commitment to the nuance of Blackness. While reading, I had to stand up, move around, walk, and signify with the text. Thank you, Shange, once again for bringing us home."

—JAMARA WAKEFIELD,
writer

DANCE WE DO

DANCE WE DO

A POET EXPLORES BLACK DANCE

NTOZAKE SHANGE

FOREWORD BY ALEXIS PAULINE GUMBS

AFTERWORD BY RENEÉ L. CHARLOW

BEACON PRESS

BOSTON

© Beacon Press
Boston, Massachusetts
www.beacon.org

Beacon Press books are published under the auspices of
the Unitarian Universalist Association of Congregations.

Text design by Nancy Koerner at Wilsted & Taylor Publishing Services

Dance We Do is published through exclusive arrangement with
The Ntozake Shange Revocable Trust

Library of Congress Cataloging-in-Publication Data

Names: Shange, Ntozake, author.
Title: Dance we do : a poet explores Black dance / Ntozake Shange ;
    foreword by Alexis Pauline Gumbs ; afterword by Renée L. Charlow.
Description: Boston : Beacon Press, 2020. | Includes bibliographical
    references.
Identifiers: LCCN 2020011359 (print) | LCCN 2020011360 (ebook) | ISBN
    9780807091876 (hardcover) | ISBN 9780807091883 (ebook)
Subjects: LCSH: African American dancers—Biography. | Dance
    companies—United States—History. | Dance and race—United States. |
    Dance—Social aspects—United States. | Shange, Ntozake.
Classification: LCC GV1785.A1 S5255 2020 (print) | LCC GV1785.A1 (ebook)
    | DDC 792.80896073—dc23
LC record available at https://lccn.loc.gov/2020011359
LC ebook record available at https://lccn.loc.gov/2020011360

CONTENTS

OUTLIVE   vii

Dance and the Eternal Life of Ntozake Shange

Foreword by Alexis Pauline Gumbs

INTRODUCTION   1

DANCE IN MY LIFE   3

FRED BENJAMIN   13

RAYMOND SAWYER   17

DIANNE MCINTYRE   23

MICKEY DAVIDSON   33

HALIFU OSUMARE   49

ED MOCK   59

An Interview with

DYANE HARVEY   63

ELEO POMARE   67

OTIS SALLID   73

An Interview with

CAMILLE A. BROWN   81

An Interview with

DAVALOIS FEARON   93

Afterword by

RENEÉ L. CHARLOW   107

Biographies of Dancers
and Choreographers   111
by Mickey Davidson

Glossary   119
*by Mickey Davidson, Dianne McIntyre,
and Halifu Osumare*

A Note from the
Ntozake Shange Revocable Trust   126

Photo Credits   129

Notes   131

OUTLIVE

DANCE AND THE ETERNAL LIFE
OF NTOZAKE SHANGE

ONCE UPON A TIME, the pages that became this book lived in a purple file folder. By the time I saw this folder it was frayed and faded by sunlight to lavender and bolstered by a protective archival sleeve in the Barnard College Archives to prevent further decay.[1] This book took a long time to emerge. The earliest versions of these pages, computer printouts of questions, interviews, and ideas, are in fact already slightly decayed. Can dance outlive paper?

If you open another folder in the same archive, you can hold a handwritten sketch of a floor plan Shange drew for her home.[2] Around the periphery of the home are the bedrooms, her own room, her daughter's room, her writing space, the kitchen, but at the very center of the home, where most folks would put the living room couch and TV, there is an open area designated in Shange's handwriting as "dance space."

Shange writes of watching her parents dance after bedtime and of practicing on the stair landings of her childhood home.[3] When Barnard College had no dance department, she worked with other students to create independent dance spaces for feedback and critique.[4] She put aside her graduate studies to dance with experimental Black dance companies in California, and when she returned to New York she prioritized attending Dianne McIntyre's dance classes with her journal in tow. She testifies that the poems would flow out over a glass of orange juice immediately after class.[5] According to McIntyre, in a conversation at Barnard in 2014, after *for colored girls who have considered suicide/when the rainbow is enuf* became a hit, Shange came right back to dance class without skipping a beat. "She was at home," McIntyre explained on stage, while Shange, sitting directly to her right, nodded her head in agreement.[6] Shange's written words, her documented practices, and the affirmation of her colleagues all show us that dance was at the center not just of her home but of her life. In fact, it would not be pushing the evidence to say that dance itself *was* Shange's truest home.

But if dance was so primary for Shange, so architecturally central to her life, why did it take so long for this book on dance to come along? Why must its publishing process outlive her like this? To make plain the plaintive question on my heart: Why are we only now reading this, after the great poet-dancer has died?

The answer is both obvious and complex. To say it succinctly, two strokes and a degenerative nerve disease got between Shange and the completion of this project.

But there is more to say.

Ntozake Shange donated the core of her archive to her alma mater right around the time they finally achieved an Africana Studies Department, a goal she had pushed for since her time at Barnard in the 1970s. And in folders alongside her notes and drafts for this book are funeral programs for several of Shange's loved ones and close colleagues.[7] She is not listed as a speaker at these funerals. It is possible that this is because during the life of this manuscript and during the passing of several of her relatives and friends she was literally not able to speak. In the same folder there are colorful charts explaining the electronics of brain activity, and a certificate of graduation, on a different grade of paper than that of her Barnard degree, from an occupational therapy program congratulating her for reteaching herself to move, to speak, to hold something in her hands.

We cannot ignore the fact that while Shange was doing the work to create this book on the significance of Black dance, gesture, and movement, she was also doing the private, almost impossible work of rebuilding and reimagining her own relationship to the physicality of her body, brain, voice, and how she could move in the world.

In an interview with Jamara Wakefield, Shange explained that she had to learn "how to eat speak read walk" again, a major obstacle for someone trying to catch up with generations of dancers to interview them.[8] However, in another way, this total rebuilding, this return to the basics of embodiment also resonates with Ntozake Shange's longer life project: How to confront that which cannot be said. How to move through that which stills the blood.[9] This is what Ntozake Shange has been teaching us with her life and work all along. Though for Shange this learning process was forced by a painful and debilitating series of strokes and a neurological disease, we cannot forget that it was Shange, with her brave poetics, her slashes and insistence that poetry must *move*, who retaught us how to speak, to read, to walk, on purpose.

Over and over again in her work, Shange uses the connection between language and movement to push each form to its limit, and to remind us that we have so much to learn.

As she says in *Lost in Language and Sound*, "That's why I dance. I can't always find the 'words' to say it. I've come to believe there are words as we know them for some things; that the body has a grammar for these constructs, which are not beyond articulation, but of another terrain. I'm becoming trans-lingual so that I may speak myself."[10]

In this way, language and movement are both queer, as in *strange*, beyond the simple grasp, forms of life that do not reproduce the world as it is but instead change it. Both language and movement are on another terrain, where Shange cannot claim facility but instead must bridge worlds in order to approach the speaking of herself. When I say *queer* here, I am not talking about the politics of sexuality in particular; I am talking about an approach to life that values the unfamiliar, awkward, and difficult as a pathway to new possibilities beyond the reproduction of the world as we already knew it. And isn't that what Shange asks for when she works to reveal the absurdity of everyday predicaments in the lives of Black women? When she breaks the boundaries of space and time to create gatherings of revolutionary ancestors, imagined children, and grown women artists healing themselves?

After a life-changing gathering of Black dancers in 1983 (including my own beloved dance teacher, the legendary Chuck Davis) at the Brooklyn Academy of Music, Shange wrote in her journal that dance is "how we remember what cannot be said."[11] And for Shange the fact that there are some things that can never be said, and that we must reach beyond what we can say, is not a problem. Or if it is a problem, it is the most worthwhile problem to have. It is a gift that she encourages us to humble ourselves to, as she encourages Black artists to move beyond a monolingual Blackness and to embrace the multilingual life of Black people across the world. For example, she turns again to dance as a practice of relearning the body that proves it is possible to relearn speech:

> As beginning dancers we have no ego problems learning merely to walk again. Hopefully we will humble ourselves to learn to simply talk again.[12]

We might think of the title character in Shange's novel *Liliane*, who seeks to learn every language that Black people have ever spoken, but her lover insists, "There's no word for us. I kept tellin' her. No words, but what we say to each other that nobody can interpret."[13]

We might think of Shange's collaborations with Nuyorican artist Adal Maldonado on *Tropicalization*, an early version of his dance protest piece *La Mambopera*, which depicts a time in Puerto Rico when African rhythms are criminalized and policed, and a dancer is brought to trial for allegedly causing a heart attack with her ancestral movements. The piece gives dance the space to short-circuit the state, declaring not only that dance can kill structures of repression but also that in its deadliness it continues to birth new life and possibility.

We could name infinite examples.

Shange's collaborative body of work encourages us to embrace the ways that Black life exceeds language, defies interpretation, and it prompts us again and again to be humble, awe-filled witnesses to the infinite blackness of the universe itself.

And yet, we cannot underestimate the painful depth of humility it took for Shange, in the middle of her life as one of the most celebrated and accomplished workers in the fields of poetry and performance, to have to relearn her own brain and body at such a basic level, to even hold a pen, to say a word, to eat a bite of food, to turn her head to listen, to struggle with dictation technologies, to shake involuntarily, to dress herself or not.

What we learn, from interviews with and public talks by Shange is that, for her, the strength to relearn came through spiritual practice. Even when she could barely move, she kept her altar, honored her ancestors, connected daily with that which is beyond the physical.[14] In other words, she practiced her faith, which was always a faith in Black movement that went beyond her individual body. It turns out that her dancing was never individual, and when she couldn't physically dance, the dance continued in her participation in community. As she says in a draft of her essay "Borders":

> Language is for me like the nectar of the living. I find it singing to me everywhere I go. I dance with Dianne McIntyre, Eleo Pomare, Mickey Davidson, Dyane Harvey and Idris Ackamoor and Cecil Taylor whenever I hear my folks speak.[15]

It doesn't take muscle coordination, or even physical mobility, for Shange to engage in collaborative dance with many of the colleagues interviewed for this book. All it takes is the speaking of the folk. During times of limited mobility, Shange would ask taxi drivers to turn to a station where she could hear some mambo, and the backseat of the cab became its own stage.[16] Dance is present because community is present, the tradition is present, the practice of linking into that which precedes, exceeds, and excites her remains possible. What forms of presence could we practice that would allow us to be in the midst of a dance collaboration no matter where we are?

Shange was engaged in a dance of multiplicity even when she was by herself. Her creative practice was in fact the spiritual work of honoring all of these selves, as she writes in her poem "fame on all fours" in *Wild Beauty*:

> *all my selves who have not yet danced*
> *my selves with no gesture/no chosen appetite*
> *no throat to scream/i must grow them out.*[17]

When she wrote these words Shange may have been talking about psychologically repressed versions of herself and even about her connection with other community members who are silenced and disenfranchised, but when we read them literally, thinking about Shange's life with disability, we can get a sense of what it takes to be a dancer and a poet in a world that largely makes dance and other forms of self-expression inaccessible to people without certain forms of physical mobility and cognitive facility.

In her conversation with Dianne McIntyre at Barnard, Shange talked candidly about how hard it was to wake up every day and remember that she could not move in the ways she had once taken for granted, remember that she would need to seek help for simple tasks. However, she said, her dance career never ended. "In my dreams I can dance," she said. "Every night I can fly."[18]

Audre Lorde kept a journal of dreams that became the source material for her poems. In her essay "Poetry Is Not a Luxury," Lorde called this "a skeleton architecture."[19] Now, "skeleton architecture" is also the name of a collective of innovative Black feminist dancers and choreographers.[20] Ntozake Shange called dance "a sculpted impulse," took a journal with her to dance class, and never stopped dreaming in dance all night long.

So where exactly is the boundary between the psychic and the physical when it comes to dance? When it comes to Ntozake Shange's eternal life as a dancer whose dance lives in the utterance of the people, the work of the spirit, the radio waves that linger in the air?

In Shange's poems, performances, and novels, revolutionary ancestors gather across time and meet in the sacred space she creates with her work. And the intergenerationality of this dance that Ntozake Shange does is part of why she dances on, not only beyond the challenges she faced in her life but also beyond her physical life itself.

In her explanatory and exploratory essay and performance "Why I Had to Dance," Shange answers the question of the dance motive on intergenerational terms. Her repeated answer to the question "why?" is "my mother."[21] In the narrative her mother is the source of her own dance practice, and dance itself becomes a type of mother, resourcing life, generating possibility.

In honor of the production of "Why I Had to Dance," choreographed by Dianne McIntyre at Oberlin College in 2012 in the midst of Shange's illness, the dancers in the piece offered their own intergenerational responses to the question of the dance motive when they gifted a series of postcards to Shange thanking her for the opportunity to embody her work.[22] Much of Shange's own relationship to dance was reflected in their responses.

"I must dance to live," said Percy Foster, reflecting Shange's insistence that dance is central, not peripheral to life. "I HAVE to DANCE, because I AM DANCE," Lawrence Lemon said, also noting that repeating the phrase "my mother" in the piece reactivated an ancestral connection for him. Likewise, Nikki Kelly wrote about dance as home, as healing. "Dance has been love to me when I needed love," said Brittany Monachino, reflecting Shange's approach to dance as an intimate resource, a place to live.

Francine Saunders offered specific gratitude for the opportunity to dance in the show because she had begun to believe that the ableism and youth focus of the field meant there was no place for her generation in the dance world. She thanked Shange for "recasting visions for my generation." And Kenya Woods reiterated the transtemporal clarity that Shange's piece made possible for her: "The work has helped awaken my dancing soul and rebirthed my spirit to move," she said. "It has allowed me to pay homage to my/our history, find the purpose of my/our future and understand the power of this moment."

In her essay "movement/melody/muscle/meaning/mcintyre," Shange analyzes the work of her teacher-turned-collaborator Dianne McIntyre as a sacred coming together. The key lesson, she tells us, is that "our lives depend on our coming together."[23]

The slash that Kenya Woods puts between "my" and "our" history, purpose, and future is part of the function of the slash in Shange's work across her career. That place where time cuts and generations come together, that place where individuality fails and multitudes emerge, that place that exceeds words. We have to dance across it.

Our lives depend on our coming together. And once again Ntozake Shange has created a space where we can be together across generations and oceans, across even that vast black cosmic space we call death. Ntozake Shange is here dancing our dreams, just like she was there at her memorial service in Washington, DC, where Dianne McIntyre silently, gracefully continued to improvise dance with Shange, where Aimee Meredith Cox presented a new dance, where a live band played mambo, and in mourning and gratitude we all jumped up out of our seats and filled the aisles dancing and embracing each other with sweat, laughter, and tears. Ntozake Shange is here because community is present. Ntozake Shange is here because we are here learning the reality of what she wrote in her elegy for Hector Lavoe and continues to teach us with this work:

> *nosotros somos an army of marathon dancers/*
> *lovers/seekers/and collectors/we have never*
> *met an enemy we can't outlive.*[24]

—ALEXIS PAULINE GUMBS, NOVEMBER 2019

DANCE WE DO

INTRODUCTION

T O REALIZE ONE HAS A BODY and to feel that
body in motion, flying, stomping, sweating, sliding, turning, cascading in somersaults, or crossing the floor in a grand chassé or a grand battement, is to
know freedom. I discovered my body late in life for a dancer,
but I have been dancing all of my life. Whatever Black people
did with our behinds and our feet I tried since I could walk.

My mother said I took after my great-aunt Marie, who
cut off her tresses in the Roaring Twenties and wore patent-
leather shoes to a funeral and shocked Augusta, Georgia. I just
wiggled and shamed everybody, just like Marie. I could have
been hers. But it was Katherine Dunham and her exquisite
care for the Black body that saved me from my wildness and
the arbitrary forms of Black vernacular dance that came so
easily to all of us, but left no traces of our history from one
generation to the next. From Haiti to Detroit, the Black people
danced. Dunham found a technique in our movement. She
found our discipline, that we had never named in our limbs,
our feet, our necks, and our torsos. Contracting, extending,

and challenging rhythm with every beat. I found by chance teachers and compatriots who were also descendants of the Dunham technique, without discussion, without so much as a word. Now it is so formal you get certificates; before, you got a well-tuned body and knowledge of the source of your power in your groin, in your thigh, in the arch of your foot. Now we can trace our movements and our desires to Syvilla Fort, Carmen de Lavallade, Judith Jamison, and Misty Copeland. There are so many Black dancers who have gone unnamed and unrecognized and hopefully we will meet some of them in this book. We are fleeting in our knowledge of who our dancers are, how hard they work, what it takes to keep a company together, what it takes to make a dance, and what it takes to make a dancer is unknown to us because we do not write it down. I have tried to capture some of this mystery, this rugged creativity that informs Black dance. I will introduce you to some of my most precious and hilarious moments with our creators, their genius, full of mirth, gravitas, and lyric. They are all of this, so individually and as a whole we create the life of a people.

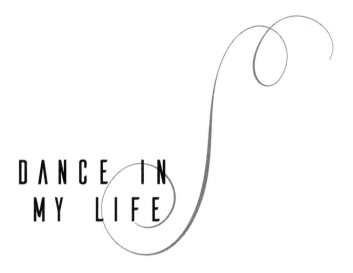

DANCE IN MY LIFE

YES, I TOOK BALLET from kindergarten through high school. Was I passionate? Never. I was always in the back row of cherubs or angels. I was never nimble or precise, and I was Black. Now, how could that be? We all know Black people can "sing and dance," so what was wrong with me? I won all the contests for best dancer at the Police Athletic League dances. I could follow a man through intricate turns and boleros till we were as one. Something was amiss. Eventually, I figured out that when my family laughed and called me "their sweet plump ballerina," and my dad told my mother that I was dancing too low-down and dirty at a party, I realized they meant that, in some sense, I was becoming a true sexual and sensual creature. No, I was not the firebird, but if Bo Diddley or Machito were being played, I was queen.

In segregated America this meant very little: our music, our dance, and our visual arts were considered natural gifts, not craft or a complicated rethinking of the possibilities of sound and the body, and I fell for it. I was a niggah, and I could do niggah dances. Not much of an accomplishment, you see. It took me years to undo this horrible stereotyped construct. I'd seen Carmen de Lavallade in *Amahl and the Night Visitors*, and I knew I would never be capable of doing what she did—I wasn't white enough. I'd see Katherine Dunham in old black-and-white movies, loved her solos, but I was ashamed of the ensemble pieces that drew from Haitian and Cuban influence. Too colored. Too sensual. Any Black person could shake that butt. So, after many years of this psychic and psychological trauma, the Black Arts Movement, as championed by Amiri Baraka and Larry Neal in the anthology *Black Fire*, gave me a new context; I was re-made.

Not only were our so-called "natchel" talents art, but they were a gift to the world, a craft, and I believe that after realizing that, something was freed in me that has changed my life dramatically. I don't even have a slave name. Paulette was afraid of her body, it could not fit, move lyrically, or get her knee to her nose in a chorus line. But when I went to the first Black Power Convention in Newark, New Jersey, in 1967, I saw authentic African, jazz, and modern dance in Black bodies of all shapes, colors, and skills, and I said with my whole being, "That's what I want to do. I want to do that." Surprisingly, the dancers invited the audience to join in, and my body knew joy in my heart. Since that time (which is before I started writing), I have searched out, studied, and worked professionally with an amazing collection of African American, African, Cuban, Brazilian, and Haitian groups. I threw myself into the world of jazz, tap, and modern dance as interpreted by Black sensibility. Those experiences, I swear to you, are among the most treasured moments of my life.

On a glorious Los Angeles day—no tremors, no mudslides or windstorms—a perfect day for an intergalactic odyssey, I had all 6'8" of Big Phil in my arms, the Great Dane at my feet, and both cats curled by my side. I woke the household with Sun Ra. Albert, the dog, started howling his own melody. Big Phil murmured, "Isn't that tonight?" I leapt around the house as if I had the Holy Ghost. The cats leapt out the window. Yes, tonight was the night Sun Ra's Myth Science Intergalactic Arkestra played in Southern California. He didn't make frequent trips to the Pacific coast, so I was beside myself. I couldn't wait to see the dancers and hear John Gilmore and Marshall Allen. I made some coffee—virtually euphoric about what was to occur. Sometimes, it was Sun Ra and his Heliocentric Arkestra, but either way it was a space defined by Black people for the world to experience on our terms.

Big Phil and I played every recording of Sun Ra we had. We were a joyous couple as we decided what to wear to a celebration of the universe. I went through my closets at least ten times. I wanted something I could move in. Big Phil decided on leather and his black velvet flowing cape. I finally chose my A-line cranberry velvet dress that Philip had given me for Christmas. We were ready once I chose a deep-red flowered scarf with gold threads running through it.

I'd seen Sun Ra and his Arkestra before at Slug's on East Third Street, when I was in school at Barnard. But I wasn't ready yet for the implications of Black people as interpreters of outer space. Now, after a year with Ed Bereal's Bodacious Buggerilla Theatre, I'd learned that one can't improvise with someone unless you respect them. Doing street theater in some of the more intriguing neighborhoods of LA increased the importance of trusting one's partner. The crowd that gathered round might be flying their colors. The crowd that gathered round, of all ages and gang affiliations, was demanding. They egged us on, trying to get us to lose our focus, but hours of rehearsal paid off. No one interrupted our work. So I learned to honor my peers for the company, found my nicest vase, and decorated it with multicolored ribbons. Then I went to the open market in Pasadena. I was gonna feed the whole Arkestra, especially the dancers: Wisteria, June, Kenneth, and whoever Sun Ra had picked from the local area.

On one of my many trips to Slug's I'd met June and Wisteria and other members of the Arkestra because the place was so small that during their breaks they had nowhere to go except mingle with the audience. My friend Cheryl Banks, who had actually begun to dance with Sun Ra, introduced me to Wisteria and June, even though we all felt like we had known each other in spirit. Even some of the guys recognized me from my many trips to Jupiter with the band. A blending of spirits held us all together and knowing one another. Many years later, when my daughter, Savannah, was about three, I carried her down the back steps of Sweet Basil's where the Arkestra was playing and had Sun Ra bless her in his fashion. He had his flowing robes and crown on. My child was mesmerized, but Sun Ra had laid hands upon her and all was right with the world. I don't know if Deadheads have the same kind of community, but there was a community that centered around Sun Ra and we were part of it.

That day Big Phil and I played every recording of Sun Ra we had. Sometimes Big Phil would join me on his alto sax. We were ebullient, Sun Ra aficionados. We loved it when Sunny would do galactic arrangements of Ellington or Basie, wearing a gold crown as befitted the interlocutor of the Universe. The band wore a mixture of contemporary clothing and traditional

African garb, always with sparklin' gold tulle over that. The dancers, who were always highlighted, wore leotards and varied scarves and the gold tulle as well, to be free to improvise.

Sun Ra was a committed Egyptologist of the kingdom of Kush. Miraculously his Arkestra was able to blend the ancient leitmotif with the most contemporary new music. Blending a panoply of African drums and electric instruments, as well as French horns, flutes, percussion instruments from the African world, and his organ, Sun Ra's sound was unmistakable.

In our "1960-something," as Baraka would say, Big Phil and I approached Dorsey High School in the heart of South Central LA. There were lots of other cars so we weren't the only ones willing to lose our breath at Sun Ra's spectacle. Musicians, sculptors, weavers, dancers, poets, professional Black Nationalists, Sunny inspired us all—made us wanna take chances.

The lights went down and suddenly the Arkestra came down the aisle singin'. I thought I was in church. The drummers made me wanna take off my clothes and celebrate the world. Finally, from out of nowhere, Sun Ra appeared at his organ downstage, sportin' his crown and a regal robe. June sang in that clear vibrant voice of hers. The drums and the organ pushed the dancers to evermore lean and defined movement. I swear, sometimes they look like Egyptian hieroglyphs caught afire. Then a film of the whole group in front of the pyramids, by the Nile in a market in Cairo, placed the group in a dialectic, from the timeless to the unknown. Then all at once the lights went out. Only drums and horns could be heard, but Sun Ra's organ, the electric guitars, and synthesizers were silent. Sun Ra had blown the circuits as well as our minds. The women kept singin' though. Technicians couldn't fix it. It was pitch black in Dorsey High. Not that we weren't pitch Black in spirit, but no light came except for undulating voices. This night changed my life. I believed the blackout was a sign from God that I was s'posed to dance. I believe that to this day.

Somehow, we all got organized and some members of the band were to stay with us, others in different parts of the city. There were no more gigs in Los Angeles, and the Arkestra had nowhere to go. It was the worst of all times for me to have company. I was finishing my independent studies for the spring semester, but I was barely started. Cultural duty was cultural duty. Naw, I couldn't. Off we went to Highland Park to our ramshackle flat, now home to nine people. I left it up to Philip to arrange who would sleep where and headed for the kitchen. I had to cook for eleven folks, then head for my study to work. But before that, I took Wisteria aside and asked her, "Where do I learn how to dance like you?" She said, "Go everywhere, learn everything," and went on her way. But I was in graduate school with another year to go. I stayed up all night writing about Black visual artists in Southern California instead. The next day I pulled myself together somehow and headed to the university. I was looking for my primary advisor, Dr. Lloyd Brown. There was something I had to do. When I found Dr. Brown, I explained I was leaving the University of Southern California.

With his usual aplomb (I'd been threatening to leave from the first day I got there), he looked at me and chuckled. "But you've only six months left to go."

"I know, but something came up that must be attended to."

"Like what?" he asked.

"Well, I want to dance with Sun Ra," I replied.

Trying not to laugh, he thought for a minute before he spoke. Then, quite energetically, he said, "I've got an idea."

"So do I," I said, a bit annoyed.

"You can finish in six months if you take both summer terms. Surely Sun Ra will still be around. You'll have your degree and still be ready to run off. Surely six months isn't too long?"

I thought for a long time; maybe Dr. Brown was trying to run a game on me. But I knew Sun Ra would be around forever. So, I confidently said, "OK. That's fair. Thank you."

I knew I had to do all that work that Wisteria had told me about. From that moment I made it my business to study with every Black dancer or choreographer I could find. "Study everywhere. Learn everything."

But nothing happened. I stayed a graduate student who haunted the stacks, surrounded by piles of *Crisis* magazines. I huddled over my journal, writing and signing "Paulette Williams" at the end of each entry or poem. I had her memories and self-conscious feelings about my body that wouldn't let me learn to fly as I'd promised. I actually had fantasies that I'd grow a tail and long ears and be a haint of the library if I continued to live the way I was living.

One day I went home and beneath the underwear on the floor I picked up a passel of papers headed by the words "Ntozake Shange." I trembled when I held the letter in my hand. I always did when I looked at a gift Ndikko and Nomusa Zaba had given me. Well, I had asked for it. I'd gone to San Francisco to visit some friends and this South African couple was explaining how one's fate was built into a name. So, all these Black people in the United States' lives were running amok because our names could not guide us. Plus it was quite the thing in Black Nationalists' circles to take on an African name to split the connection to slavery, to be free. I had another reason as well. I was a feminist as well as a nationalist and wanted to be rid of "Paulette," which was a diminutive of Paul, my father's name. So I asked Ndikko to name me. He said he'd have to observe me for months, maybe even a year, before he'd know what my name was to be. It was about seven months before Ndikko said to me as we crossed the Golden Gate Bridge that he had my name: "Ntozake Shange," "she who comes with her own things/who walks like a lion." So I put the papers with all the various nuances of my new name away and went to play with the dog.

Still I longed to dance and sun in peculiar patterns, and racing up the street gave me an outlet once in a while. In one of my jaunts, I promised that if I ever left Los Angeles, I'd just introduce myself as Ntozake, as if that was in fact who I was. Then I could be or do anything I wanted because I had nothing to hold me back, and that's what I did. I signed my name Ntozake Shange at the Black Artist Collective roster in Boston.

Now. I could be a dancer. I could be anything.

This small book pays homage to my remarkable teachers, the discipline of the companies I worked with, and the musicians who were our partners in this driven and focused art form. Hopefully, you'll have some sense of the Black dance community. Our concern is that there were never any reviews of the work we executed. There is no documentation of the techniques of these unique artists who will leave this world having left their knowledge and love of dance in their bodies. No graduate students came to trace the opus of these masters. So, on the internet, at the library, in the dance magazines, Black dance doesn't exist yet. It's still just "natchel," what we can do 'cause "we colored." We are "colored." Dance we do. But how we dance. Come with me for memories of decades in the vital and overlooked Black dance world. We will make you do those barrel turns, leaps, and pirouettes, and we will dance that dance till there's no breath left in us and we have love in our hearts. It's too beautiful; only a dead man won't smile. It was true the whole time we do sing and dance. Oh how we dance.

FRED BENJAMIN

A SMALL CROWD of brightly clad folks gathered by the door to the studio. Some in leotards and tights, others in knit body wraps or classic leggings intended to induce sweat. They hovered by the tape recorder and the passel of tapes. Names like Minnie Ripperton, Grace Jones, Lou Rawls, Michael Jackson, and Blind Lemon Jefferson, drew "oohs and ahs" from the dancers moving themselves to rhythms, unnamed melodies, and random beats encouraging free movement. Outside the animated music-focused groups, there were isolated hips and shoulders, warming up doing first- and second-position pliés, jazz port de bras. A weight-lifted backstretch in the corner. There were bodies in motion or sculpted tension everywhere you looked. The dancers by the doors started moving across the studio with élan and discipline, staking out the space for their bodies to articulate themselves. A slim, long, red-yellow man walked through the separating class as students took their places. Fred Benjamin, the leader, started the music, and without a word began dancing his warm-up, letting the class catch up. He lyrically explored space while challenging the dancers' muscle memory and careful eyes to create. These beginning phases of a dance served as a movement blending the disparate bodies into one breath, one aesthetic, one impulse. Always sleek as Benjamin's body thrust through the class of dancers, reflecting his every gesture, the front line, usually professionals, brought style and energy to the jazz fragments' parallel feet, knees bent legs, perpendicular arms, flat backs, and a Fred Benjamin warm-up had commenced.

Benjamin's movements demonstrated inescapable sensuality. The most casual hand gesture had a come-hither air to it. The stretches lured the shortest bodies to heights daring a would-be Judith Jamison to present herself. After familiarity with the movements, the class divided, so that the back three lines came forward and the front line moved to the back, allowing everyone to get a good look at what Fred was up to. Sporting an isolated torso and shoulders, he led us in jazz pirouettes and other erotically precise movements that coaxed us to quickly glide across the floor.

This is the first portion of the warm-up, which left everyone aware of the sensual attributes of their bodies. The last line of the performers led gender-fluid dancers to rollick with battements and their pirouettes to soar. Going across the floor, the rest of us proceeded with our more modest battements and attitudinal apogee, which lent drama to the moment. Finally, leaps, barrel turns, and marches of plié relevé led to dance runs until everyone in the cast was breathless, ready for the real work of the combination executed by groups of four or five so individuals could be observed, encouraged, and directed. The class ended with rapid second-position plié turns on a diagonal, ending with enormous applause for Fred Benjamin, who took his bow at the end of the class, freeing the bodies or any type of rigid hips sway as bosoms bounce, arms embrace the unseen other, and every movement sweats.

I knew Benjamin recognized me because I was a regular for the two-thirty class. I sat in the third-row center so I could really see him, without having to compete with the professional dancers in the front line. It was the first class I took after having my baby. I remember distinctly that I had lost so much weight that I didn't recognize myself. Fred didn't either. He waved me to the front line, assuming I could keep up, which I could. Like a colored butterfly after the final pirouette that ended with fingers singularly placed on the rear of the shoulder one by one. I saw Fred smiling at me, nodding his head, yes yes. What a day that was. To search out affirmation I danced with a new kind of confidence after that, leaving me to concentrate on my attitude and breath instead of my steps. Now I moved more like a cat or, larger still, an ocelot.

RAYMOND SAWYER

YOU WOULD NOT IMAGINE a short stocky young man as a dancer until he strode across the room toward you and his legs became telephone poles or huge redwood trees. Raymond Sawyer floated across space as if he were a heron. His arms took on the character of cypress tree limbs, cutting through the air casually but with grandeur. There was something graceful about his movement. Elegant and African. Even without the many drummers who accompanied the class, Raymond's body took on the alternating contractions and stretched. That was characteristic of his many combinations across the floor. Amazingly, Raymond consistently made loud clicking sounds with his tongue that hovered over the drums, becoming the primary rhythm that we danced to. This clicking sound caused Raymond's head to dart like a lizard or a snapping turtle. With an open chest always, Raymond propelled himself and the class to many movements based on the Horton or Dunham technique. We took to looking like we were straight from Lagos once we got started. And Raymond mixed popular dance moves with classic Dunham poses. Raymond was a third-generation Katherine Dunham dancer, so his work had meaning because he was trained by someone whom Dunham trained, and he was serious that we aspire toward that excellence and particularity of the Dunham technique. Arched feet and second-position relevé with arching back while holding on to the bar was one of Raymond Sawyer's favorite positions. He would glide down the row as we stretched in torment until he got to the end, then he would whisper, "Now come down," and you could hear the sighs of relief as we let loose our arched feet and flattened them on the floor with aplomb. After a thoroughly Dunham and Horton ballet bar, Raymond took to the floor and we began pelvic exercises that challenged every muscle from your crotch to your navel. We shook as if we were trying to propel 1966 Ford transmissions from our torsos to our toes. Sawyer's other favorite floor exercises were leg lifts on a slow count of sixteen, relying on your legs to be perpendicular to your hips, until your ankles were an inch off the planks and you could see your thighs tremble and feel the arch in your feet begin to ache. Coming across the floor Raymond encouraged improvisation after he had done grand battements, pirouettes, and boogaloos. They were now as familiar to us as natural nighttime entertainment and made into more formal but groovy dance combinations. We carried on from corner to corner, picking up speed and pungency as we followed one another in diagonal lines.

Raymond used to love to have parties, and it was as if the resident dance class had simply moved to his front room. When in leotards and other outrageous outfits, we experimented stylistically with Raymond's staccato contraction-release-contraction-release demi-plié, hip to hip teasing as he enticed us physically to respond to him. We could raid his closets for costumes to dramatize our movements. Once he entered the large dancing space in a silken cape and crown, being carried gently by the male dancers of the group. He looked like an emperor as the women dancers danced below the cape and carried it higher toward the ceiling so that we became like a parade of Black and Filipino bodies on the Divisadero Street: Raymond Sawyer's Afro-American Dance Company. Out the front door we would go, making strange grunts and howls as we dared the street people or the police to halt our caravan. Down the hill, toward Minnie's Can-Do Club and the all-night breakfast deli where we would relax and in-vibe. Raymond Sawyer's dance classes were a way of life that took charge of one's days and nights, leaving the body exhausted, muscles aware and in good form till the next time.

Sometimes we met at Potrero Hill or in other neighborhoods. Raymond's Afro-American Dance Company made itself known as we engaged in dance guerrilla theater, taking on pedestrians and shoppers as they went about their daily tasks. Our daily task was to make dance a part of their environments. With drummers accompanying us and Raymond's clicking tongue, we tore up San Francisco streets, making Golden Gate Park as close to an ordinary New Orleans Mardi Gras arena as possible for twenty to forty dancers of color could.

When Raymond passed away, we used to have concert dance performances of his longer pieces. We were in the company of Black, Latinx, and Asian terpsichores such as Elvia Marta, Cecilia Marta, Brenda Miller, Rosalie Alphonso, and Paula Moss. I discovered a coterie of friends who shared my passion of dance and friendship. It was from the bevy of a Moulin Rouge chorus line that I found the first dancers who would improvise my poetry. I will never forget being at San Francisco State University in a huge auditorium reading the poem "between a dancer and poet." Rosalie appeared at the end of the hall and improvised her way down the center aisle, a perfection of Horton attitude turns and leg lifts, with great drama, beautiful extension, and arched back till she reached me and we began a Raymond Sawyer improvisation and combination that we had been working on. It was a glorious day, that drew unexpected applause from the audience. Rosalie was the first Filipina in the *for colored girls* troupe; she made our company dazzle with her light-footedness and her fearless glance. Paula Moss and Elvia Marta were key principals in the original *for colored girls*. Paula brought the show with me back to the East Coast to Studio Rivbea for the Alternative Jazz Festival in 1974. Raymond Sawyer trained all of us, and you could tell by our erect heads, perfect posture, and turnout that we took him seriously.

Paula Moss mentioned that Raymond Sawyer demanded we keep our chests open. He implored us to own our bodies and own the movement, letting us know that we were entitled to dance, that we were allowed to perform, because our bodies were stronger than we knew. We could take on movements and forms that seemed to be beyond our muscle strength, but if we pushed ourselves, we could do it. Raymond gave us the courage to manifest our ideas, which culminated in *for colored girls who have considered suicide/when the rainbow is enuf.* There he lent us theater lights and costumes, and offered the dance studio as rehearsal space for us. His support was absolutely essential to our success. We were Raymond Sawyer dancers trained and inescapable.

Paula reminded me that Raymond's signature piece was to the O'Jays' "For the Love of Money," where he had us dancing on multiple levels with the company coming and going from the stairs at different points in time. There was always more than one string of dancers on the stage, each doing a different kind of movement, so they complemented and punctuated one another. The other thing was that Raymond, as a gay man comfortable with his sexuality, empowered female dancers to discover our sexuality and sensuality both personally and in dance. We came to love our hips and the curve of our asses, and to use them in a way to accentuate our femininity. Raymond used drummers a lot, but he also used his clicking tongue always.

Raymond thought he was never recognized for his brilliance. He was on fire when he came to San Francisco, and we always filled his classes until it was hard to find space to lift one's leg. There were several manifestations of Raymond's frustration with not being recognized. One of the manifestations of his frustration was to have us do things for him. I used to drive him around to engagements and rehearsals across the Bay Area at Everybody's Dance Studio or the Oakland Ensemble Theatre. Paula Moss used to have to clean his rooms. We had to know, and he let us know that it was a privilege to study with him and it was especially an honor to dance with him.

When Raymond left San Francisco he traveled the West Coast before moving to Australia, where he worked with burgeoning aboriginal dance companies. With great enthusiasm and creativity, he took into account the traditions and movements of aboriginal culture while charging it with what Raymond called "vernacular African American dance," which he insisted was as particular as Afro-Cuban dance or traditional

Haitian dance. The plague that decimated the dance community finally caught up with Raymond. AZT and the other miracle drugs stopped working, and Raymond began to die. Yet, he went about his daily life as normal, simply letting everyone around him know that he was dying. He accepted it, but he was going to live until his last breath. He shall be sorely missed.

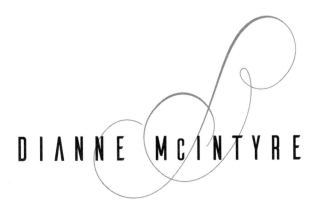

DIANNE McINTYRE

ONE SUMMER NIGHT, at the East in Brooklyn I was dancing wildly to somebody's music when I was joined by a woman whose muscles screamed discipline and whose movements suggested something I'd never seen before. As I fell to the side of the wall, she introduced herself as Bernadine Jennings. We became fast friends, dancing anywhere we could, with whomever we could. Bernadine changed my life. She introduced me to the Clark Center, where not only did Fred Benjamin and Alfred "Pepsi" Bethel teach, alongside Charles Moore and Loremil Machado, but Titos Sompa and Mercedes Baptista explored movement and welcomed students. With Bernadine's guidance, I found myself studying with all of them.

One day Bernadine said there was a young woman in Harlem who was holding auditions for a new dance company. Bernadine thought I should try out. I hesitated, and Bernadine said they might have more technique, but they haven't got your spirit. Go ahead and try. So, I did.

In the 1970s, 125th and 1st Avenue was bleak and forlorn,

and I searched high and low for a dance studio. To my cha-grin, all I found was a methadone clinic and a church. Finally, I turned around, almost giving up hope when I saw a sign pointing to the second floor of the methadone clinic where the name Dianne McIntyre was displayed. I knew that was where I was supposed to go.

NTOZAKE SHANGE: Who do you consider to be among your mentors?

DIANNE MCINTYRE: Elaine Gibbs [Redmond]. She was my first dance teacher in Cleveland. I was four when I started, and I continued through my early high school years. I didn't realize it then, but she was *the* singular dance teacher for Black children in Cleveland. I don't think we could have gone anyplace else because of seg-regation. She took my love of dance and made me love it more. Through her, I associated dance with grace, beauty, elegance, dignity, pride and joy. She was an elegant woman and was so gentle and kind while teach-ing us. She showered all her students with such love, such caring. What I received from her was the message that "I can do it—whatever" in dance. She instilled that in me. She took us to see the most brilliant ballet com-ing through Cleveland. We saw *Billy the Kid* by Eugene Loring. When I met the dancers backstage all I could talk about was the choreography, especially the open-ing, "Going West." I wanted to make dance like that! I was about thirteen at the time.

My father, F. Benjamin "Benny" McIntyre, . . . taught me ballroom dancing and all of the popular dances from his youth in the 1930s. Over the years, in my

choreography, a signature is my use of the "vernacular" or social dances in my formal choreography. My
father—when he could dance—was a smooth ballroom
dancer. He could spin, glide, and dip, moving swiftly
across the floor. Very suave. Over the years, guys always
liked dancing with me because I was a good "follower"
or good collaborator on the dance floor. A good partner.
We could try anything, and it would work. I picked
that up from my father. Maybe that somewhat relates
to my desire to collaborate with other artists as a
choreographer.

I went past the sniffling junkies and the weakened steps until
I found Studio A. Once I opened the door, I knew I was safe.
Dancers lined the walls; there was a pianist and a drummer,
and some women at a table with pieces of paper. Somebody
gave me a piece of paper with a number on it. I just got in line
like the rest of them and waited for my number to be called. I
kept looking around at all the other dancers, who seemed so
professional and so self-confident; I began to wonder about
myself and what made me think I was ready for this level of
dance. Anyway, I was in the line already. . . . I had a number,
and I would do my best.

So, when my turn came up, I did a combination, twice,
without missing a beat, and went back to my place. Then they
started calling out numbers. My heart was beating fast, and I
felt my legs weaken, but my number wasn't called. I was still
in the room with fewer dancers, but they were formidable. We
got invited to do another combination. Once again I did it,
twice on the left and once on the right. My pirouettes got confused; they went the wrong way, but I did turn and manage
to get back to first-position plié like everybody else. Finally,

there was a section where we were instructed to improvise thirty-two counts. I was scared to death because that was a long time. But I said, "Well hell, I am here," and we began. I danced my heart out, and scared as I was, all I could do was keep myself standing up and not crying. Then suddenly, while I was in this virtual stupor, I heard my number being called. I was sure I should get ready to leave, but the voice began to congratulate us as new members of Sounds in Motion Dance Company. That's how I met Dianne McIntyre.

NTOZAKE SHANGE: Was there a moment when you realized that you had to dance or choreograph for the rest of your life?

DIANNE MCINTYRE: It was in my third year in college, when I was majoring in French while also taking the dance major courses on the side. Something happened inside of me. I can't remember what, but I pledged to dedicate my life to dance. I do remember being affected by studying dance history in the dance department and learning about cultures of non-Western societies, mostly in Asia and Africa. When I realized the power and importance the dancer had in those societies as the people who communicated with the deities, kept the communal vitality of the people going, continued the history, and embodied the rituals, I realized that to be a dancer was not a frivolous thing. I learned that, through dance, I, too, could help bring those gifts to my community. After that, I went for it.

I moved to New York in 1970 and began taking dance classes around town. In 1971 I started studying with Gus Solomons Jr., who shortly after invited me to work with his company. In fact, I was in his first company. It was through Gus that I learned how to rehearse choreography in a professional setting, where you are committed to work from 8:30 a.m. to 2 p.m. every day. I learned the protocol, the trial and error, the building of the piece, the editing, the pairing up people, offering the right movement for the right body or right abilities to make one shine. I learned that you need humor, patience, a mechanism so the dancers aren't worried about your administrative problems. What I really learned from Gus was persistence in expanding an individual's performance capabilities. For a choreographer, this is essential. Even if you have the greatest dancers, can they do your work, specifically? So, through Gus working with me, I not only expanded into his style; I expanded into truly being a "dancer," a professional-level dancer. I blossomed.

Sounds in Motion was her baby and she was the primary judge. To my surprise, I was a scholarship student for Sounds in Motion. That meant I had to clean up the floors and windows, but I wouldn't have to pay for the class, which I couldn't miss. What joy, what freedom, to be able to say I belonged to a group of people whose primary objective in life was to dance. I had found a home at last.

NTOZAKE SHANGE: Are you willing to share your "process" as a choreographer?

DIANNE MCINTYRE: Hmm. Process. This is not that easy to decipher within myself, but I'll try. If I am working with spoken word as an inspiration, road map, or as something that will happen simultaneously to the dance, I study those words until they are in my body. If the words are a guideline, then I try to envision how the author would have seen this in dance. I also did that when working with Duke Ellington's "Deep South Suite," which had a very specific programmatic theme as written by Ellington in his program notes. Choreographing to that music, I tried to create the moves that Ellington would have created. I tried to have the dancers be other instruments in his band. If there was a rest in the music, maybe he meant that for a dance move. The dance was not to parrot or "mickey-mouse" the music, but to be an additional voice, another layering to the music.

Sometimes I might interpret the words as energy in the dancer's body rather than a literal translation. Sometimes the dance is a commentary on the words or on the character. Sometimes the dance is the character come to life in the movement and offering you additional information the words did not say. In other words, with recorded music or text I try to collaborate with the other artist even if they are not there.

When working with live music, I try to create the dance *as* the music is being composed by the composer or musician. When I hear something that inspires a certain movement, the composer then sees that and responds by creating something audible based on the movement. Back and forth like that. The dancers and the other musicians must be alert and keep up with us because the process can be very fast. In working with a composer creating together like this, both of us are the boss and both of us are the non-boss. We are equal. Equal in the original idea and equal in the creative process. I also work in improvisation with dance and music together. The process here is that the dancers and musicians are all a part of the "band." They all play off each other—within whatever structure is set. It takes a lot to train dancers to work in this way. They must be able to hear the nuances in the music and think of their body as a musical instrument playing with one another or several other instruments— dancers and musicians.

I also like to create works in silence. I am influenced by the rhythm that can be "heard" in the silence, or the stark imagery created by a number of bodies interacting together in space.

I met my dear friend Mickey Davidson at the same audition. She was a scholarship student too. We had the energy but not yet the technique to be in the first company. But that did not bother me at all. All I had to do was learn, and learning is such a pleasure. I took Dianne McIntyre's classes and understudied at rehearsal eagerly, and there was no end to the surprise of what the human body could do. Dianne's dance was predicated on the breath, so that eventually the sounds of breathing fiercely or gently became our music.

NTOZAKE SHANGE: Does your work directly relate to Black and African American people? Does it connect to the experiences and the culture?

DIANNE MCINTYRE: My work is related to African Americans. Even though when I was a child I just loved to dance and wasn't dancing to relate to any culture or situation, as I grew and became tuned into the energies around me, the influence of other artists, world situations, and my own love of Black music, my choreographic work started reflecting those influences.

NS: How so?

DM: Most of the music I connect to my work is by Black composers, even if the dances do not have an African American theme or narrative. However, the influence of the music energizes the dance in a way that could be called culturally specific. Sometimes I have built dances based on African American history or emotions arising out of the content expressed by the dancer who most often—to date—is Black. As well, I might incorporate some music that is from our social/party/fun dancing, or from dancing our rituals. I also choreograph works for groups that are racially integrated or primarily white. In this case I am still bringing to the creative process, even without intention, those influences that have become my trademarks, many of which could be identified as African American: ritual/spiritual element, dynamic use of energy, rhythmic nuances, triumphant finales, social dance elements, interplay with live music, non-Western logic in structure. Some of my works have been on the soft edge of activism, related to the "Black experience."

What my work is not is some identifiable movements that for some reason or another have become associated with "Black dance." As many see, there is more and more diversity in the field among Black choreographers because as the dance field expands, there are more schools of training and more ways choreographers have chosen to express themselves. In the early days, because of limitations in where we were allowed to train, some choreographers created works that were derivative of the early great African Americans who were pioneers in the dance field: Alvin Ailey, Katherine Dunham, Pearl Primus, Talley Beatty, Donald McKayle. At one time it was assumed that if you were Black and a choreographer, your dance moves had to look something like one of those to qualify as a true dance of Blacks. Now the voices are so varied and often have no direct training connection to the schools of those pioneers.

NS: Does the history of Black dance influence your work? Do you find it important to incorporate traditional movements from antebellum American dance, minstrels, tap vernacular?

DM: I have a love of history. I have a love of dance. Therefore, they have merged in my work. I include our vernacular dance in my work, and I cannot say why from a philosophical, educational, or sociological reason. Because of growing up dancing the dances with my friends and finally learning the dances done before I was born, these things are just in me. So, when I create, they come out. When people have seen this in my work they have called for me to recreate old historical dances for the stage and film. As a result, I have gained more knowledge of these dances from researching these particular projects. So, this has become one of the areas I am known for. I love it, and this historical dance and

today's social dance [are] what bridges us back to our
roots in this country, in Africa, in the Caribbean, and
throughout the diaspora. For me, it's just in my body—
so why deny it?

To my surprise, Bernadine sauntered through the doors, gave
Dianne a big hug, and waved at me. It turned out that Bernadine was one of Dianne's primary dancers. I had a lot to learn.

Shoooooowah Shooowah aaaaaaaahhhhhh uuuummmmm-
mmmph uuuuuuumph.

These are not the random sounds of the wind on the prai-
rie or the hush of the subway. The slight, muscular woman in
the front of the dance studio facing 125th Street on a bright
Saturday afternoon began the intermediate class of improvisation and modern dance.

MICKEY DAVIDSON

I MET MICKEY DAVIDSON at auditions for Sounds
in Motion Dance Company in East Harlem in
1973. Thanks to Bernadine Jennings I found out
Dianne McIntyre was holding auditions for her new dance
company on East 125th Street and 1st Avenue on a Saturday
afternoon. I was terrified about auditioning for a professional
dance company in New York, but I thought I was ready, and
I desperately wanted to dance. I got myself together and took
the eastside train to 125th and 1st Avenue and marched myself
up 1st Avenue. To my surprise, I was afraid I had come to
the wrong place. How could a dance company full of vivacity,
life, and joy be in such a dreary place? I wondered how I was
going to get past all the junkies. This can't be right; this can't
be where they are. But I found it and went up the two stories
to the floor where I heard the piano and saw figures in tights
and leotards and leg warmers tuning up their bodies, chatting
on the stairs. I went up and up until I got to the room where I
saw some women sitting at a table with pencils and papers. I
went up to the table and took one of the pads of paper. I wrote

my name and put my experience and left it with the woman, and went to warm up with the others.

I was sort of introverted at first. I didn't know if the other girls were experienced and knew it all, or if they were as nervous as I was. I was quiet and took my place on the stairway waiting for things to begin.

I noticed a young woman not much taller than me with thick legs and short cropped nappy hair coming up the stairs with a little boy behind her. I wondered what she was going to do with a child at the tryouts, but then I figured she must know what she was doing or she wouldn't have brought him. She walked by me with great élan. I said, "Well, you never know," and I wished her good luck.

NTOZAKE SHANGE: So, while you were living life as an artist with a son to take care of, what did you discover about dance and yourself?

MICKEY DAVIDSON: I discovered that I had to do it. That was the only thing that made consistent sense to me. People didn't expect much of me in terms of acquiring greatness, not only as a dancer but also as a person; I found this out later on in life. Being a mother and being responsible for another human being made the search for dance and the functionality of dance that much more urgent. Dance was my vehicle for paying bills and providing a home. I could have settled for being a good teacher as advised, but since very young I knew I had to perform first. Having the responsibility of motherhood put a certain level of urgency into me being committed to developing a dancing voice as my vehicle for being a parent, a provider, and myself.

I heard the piano start and the clap of two hands, which was Dianne signaling it was time for the process to commence. Once inside the room I heard Dianne begin to welcome us and say how pleased she was that we were interested in working with her and that she was sorry she couldn't take all of us, but there were only ten places available, and there were at least fifty of us there, if not more. She said that we would go through several combinations and she would pick the dancers she felt would fit most easily into her group and her style, and she thanked us all for trying. Then we went to warm up, with her leading the exercises. The woman I had seen come in with the little boy was not far from me. But she smiled at me, I smiled at her, and that made me feel a little better. That was the first smile of the day. I hadn't seen my friend Bernadine yet. But once we started moving, I saw her waltz through the door and begin to inspect us all as we did the exercise. They weren't too hard, the exercises—the rond de jambe, jeté and assemblé, pirouettes on both sides, grand battements, port de bras, modern and ballet mixed so that the body was heated up and pliable by the time we were finished.

There was a man with long dreadlocks playing the piano; they were uneven, the dreadlocks. And they grew from different sides of his head, so it was quite odd looking, but the piano he played was mournful and at other times playful, so we were always kept alert while doing the exercises, which could become routine. Then Bernadine went around the room and gave us different numbers with numbers 1–5 with all the 1's going to one group, and all the 2's going to another group, and so on. I was in number 4, so I met all the 4's. There were six of us.

Then I saw that the young woman with the son had placed him in a corner with some cars, and he was amusing himself.

She was in group 5 and I was in group 4, so we were close to each other and urging each other on with crossed fingers for good luck. At first, we did three or four steps, a slide, a turn, an apogee and attitude, and a small jump. Then they were done hurriedly, and they were done on the balls of our feet. As with any audition, combinations became more and more difficult as we went through them. Bernadine and another woman would go through the room and tap us on the shoulder, which meant that you were dismissed and hadn't made the cut this time.

I lasted and lasted, and finally, there were only about fifteen of us left, and I was still there. Hanging in there doing the steps, and so was the woman with the child. So, I just kept trying. I was sweating and trying, and I lasted until there were only ten of us. I crossed my fingers and I could hear my heart pounding. I kept thinking, "Oh my God, I hope I make it. I am almost there." And then I didn't feel anybody touch my shoulder, and then there were three of us. I said to myself, "Oh my God, they're only going to pick one of the three. Oh, my goodness, I made it this far; this is good enough," and the girl with her son was still there too. And she was sweating and smiling, too, and so we all three were standing there. There was silence and there were no more exercises. And Dianne and Bernadine were staring at us. They asked us to walk across the floor in a dance walk. So, we walked the floor in a dance walk. Then we had to figure out a movement to present ourselves and come forward and say our names and what city we were from, where we had studied, and who we danced with. So, when it was my turn, I said I was zake shange from San Francisco, California, because I had just left San Francisco and come to New York and I thought I was all Miss West Coast. Then I said I studied with Raymond Sawyer, Ed Mock, and Halifu Osumare. I felt like that was a whole lot of training altogether, so I felt very proud. I heard the other two girls say where they were from, but I was so nervous I blocked everything out except listening for what Dianne and Bernadine were going to say next.

And then I heard Dianne get up from the table come to each of us and say welcome. She welcomed the other two as members of the company and I was a scholarship student. She was delighted to have us and saw great promise among us. And we were all going to be with her. Then she introduced herself to us, and we introduced ourselves to each other. We gave each other big hugs.

Then we proceeded to get dressed again, because there were no showers, and went downstairs, past the junkies, to walk down 125th Street after some good summer afternoon sweat and three or four hours of dance.

I found out the woman whose son I had been watching all afternoon was named Mickey Davidson. We became fast friends and were always at rehearsal and class together. It turned out that Mickey was taken into the first company and I was in the second company because I had not had as much training as she had. The third girl who was taken was Francine. She was long and lithe while Mickey and I were short and stocky, but all three of us were buoyant with joy at being taken into the company.

I learned more about Mickey Davidson over the months and years. She lived in an apartment on the Lower East Side that was a proverbial Lower East Side apartment, with the tub in the kitchen and two bedrooms that were filled with bunk beds. There was a room with an office and a desk for keeping notes and files for keeping track of the business that she ran. She had two dance companies, one that had traditional African American dance and one that did tap. She was also developing one that did swing. That was one way she earned her living, and it helped her keep her craft at its peak as well as her son by her side.

MICKEY DAVIDSON: I was one of the first five students that started the Venettes Cultural Workshop with the founder-director, Mary Baird, in Wyandanch, Long Island[, New York]. This was the major turning point in my life. During my training, I studied ballet, tap, charm, and jazz. From the original five, I was the only one to turn professional. Now I have to get more personal as to why this time in my life was such a major turning point on my road to become a dancing performer.

After running away from home at fifteen, I negotiated living at Mrs. Baird's house. After being on the streets and experiencing real life, you can't go back home with your parents as an innocent teenager. And by sixteen, I had a baby son that I refused to give up for adoption or put into foster care. I was not allowed to bring my child into my parents' home, that's why it was so important living with Mrs. Baird and her family, including her daughter Vanessa, who has carried on the legacy of her mother. The Venettes were the first group I performed with using live music. Working with that company was also how I got my first taste of improvising in performance, dancing with Bobby, a dancer Mary brought in from the Bronx. Not only did I improvise to survive a mental blackout, but I did my first ace in the hole [a popular Lindy Hop air step]. By the time I was seventeen, I [had] found peace, purpose, strength, and optimism for life in the music of jazz.

NTOZAKE SHANGE: After you decided you had to dance, where did you go first?

MD: I attended the University of Illinois Champaign-Urbana as a dance major. It was mainly my experiences outside the department that shaped my future in African American dance forms. College helped me connect the history, culture, politics, the storytelling, and hope found in the jazz music and how to move to it. I came to understand, when I became a professor, why so many freshmen came to dance class first semester, because that's where they felt safe, you know how things work in a studio. I trained. You know, I mean, it was about training, it was about networking, the buzz, about being a part of an intergenerational dance community. It was about being read in terms of what I was good at but what I needed to work on.

NS: Explain to me the idea of being read.

MD: Being read is being critiqued very critically but also lovingly. It is critical because it's real. I have one hip, my left hip, slightly turned in right, when the other is turned out. Technically, that is not the kind of body that I am supposed to have as a dancer. You could be a good teacher, but I was choosing to perform. I was guided into teaching. Teaching was a part of my life early on, but I felt to be a good teacher I needed to live my life as an artist. Then I'd have something to really give. Thelma Hill would come to our Sounds in Motion performances. She would say I was a good performer but never a good dancer. I really wanted to hear that, but

the standard for technically dancing was high. I didn't
have that type of body, but people watched me when I
danced, I believe, because they could feel my truth [this
is what I needed to do], and I grew to accept myself as a
performer who danced.

This was the only thing that I enjoyed doing that
made sense to me in the world. There was something
about dance, a truth about my own physical brilliance,
limitations, and growth.

I had so much to learn. . . . She knew so much about different
kinds of Black dance and the history of it. And the dancers
who did them. She knew the female Silver Belles, who were
Black chorus girls from the '30s or '40s, and the Copasetics,
who were a smooth tap dance troupe in the '30s and '40s.
They were still performing even when I met Mickey in the
1970s. Mickey did tap and swing and the jitterbug. She was
just amazing; she was a treasure trove of Black history and an
awful lot of fun.

On the other hand, she was an improviser, like I wanted
to be. I wanted to dance freely and feel the impulse to have
my body do what I wanted it to do to the music I heard. She
danced with Sun Ra and Cecil Taylor and seemed to climb
the piano as his fingers trolled the keys. She walked on the
air upside down and around. The audience would make these
magical sounds that were as thick as John Henry's arms. Or
delicate like Carmen de Lavallade fingers. Mickey's body
could keep up with all of them and bring to mind any one of
those images, in rhythm and in tune.

MICKEY DAVIDSON: It was around 1984 when I saw the
Norma Miller Dancers at the Village Gate in New York.

I knew two of the performers who were going to be my way in. This was a major change and artistic bonding with my art, my people, and myself. This connected my studies in college with the music, dances, and history of African Americans from the Deep South. The energy, the relationship to the music, and the joy it brought to the audience touched my center. The fact that this is a form of dance accessible to all people, not just for professionals, made it right for me. I approached Amaniyea Payne and Clyde Wilder from the African dance community to find out where and when the group worked out, and I remembered about the counting thing. I came into the rehearsal and there were Norma, Frankie Manning, Chazz Young, Stormy and Darlene Gist, and Billy Rector. I acted like I had never danced before. I didn't tell them I was a professional dancer. I went to go get their coffee, and when they found out I had a car, I would take people home and it got people to show you something. In between rehearsals, I would look at footage at the dance library at Lincoln Center. I recognized steps from my Venette Cultural Workshop days. One day at Roseland Ballroom I had followed the group, and one of the ladies didn't show up. I got to work the gig Norma had with the Basie Orchestra, and she looked at me and said, "OK, it's time for you to go on." She gave me her leotard and a scarf that was put around my waist, and I hit "Jumpin' at the Woodside." It was quite a baptism. It was a link.

Finally, my craft as a poet moved along so well that I was getting jobs, and once more I wanted to work with a dancer, and what better dancer to work with than Mickey, with whom I danced myself. I asked Mickey if she would consider working with me and the poems when I had jobs, and we would set the fee depending on how much the door paid. She agreed, and a forty-year relationship began.

NTOZAKE SHANGE: You know what I was just thinking? I was just thinking Savannah was in one of your classes.

MICKEY DAVIDSON: The children's class I developed as part of Sounds in Motion's presence in Harlem [1976–1983] was important to me. When the class was dropped, that really hurt. I had found a place to invest in teaching. This is why it was important to me and how Savannah fit in. The children's classes at Sounds in Motion Dance Studio was a miniature concept of what we did as adults. We improvised; we trained in dance, but we had live music. We had Mr. Hank Johnson, who was a composer and pianist who worked with Martha Graham and José Limón, in terms of contributing compositions. By the time he was with us, he was kind of worn out dealing with the business of the art, but not tired of being artistic. He was excellent for the children and for me. To me, a highlight was that the children knew how to improvise on their own and extend the introduction of the song in order to get into place. Mr. Hank followed them perfectly because they were musically at the right place to start the melody.

Another time we were doing one of the studio workshop presentations. You know how everybody laughs with children because they're so cute? Kisha, one of the students, stopped and said, "There's nothing cute about this. I am dancing." They were very serious students learning the Sounds in Motion concept of movement with music. Savannah was three and a half and still carrying her bottle. You brought her in, and I told you, "Mothers could not come into the studio, but the bottle could." It only took three classes before the bottle was put down and she joined the other students. Peer teaching is very powerful. All the children took the one-and-a-half-hour class as serious as the adult class that came after them. Today, your Savannah has her PhD; Kim Holmes is one of the leading house hip-hop people and teaches nationally and internationally. Kisha Bunridge is a playwright and has had several pieces produced at the National Black Theatre Festival and the Crossroads Theatre. I've been able to follow these young ladies as they have grown and developed, even after being their dance teacher. But they will always be my girls.

At first, we did a few poems, say five or six, and eventually, it got to the point where I was doing fifteen to twenty poems, and Mickey would dance eight to ten of them. She would take solos in silence as well, and then we were really on a roll. We stayed away from the poems in *for colored girls* because people had heard them already and had fixed notions of what the movements should look like, having seen them on stage once before in choreopoem form. So, Mickey and I liked to keep them guessing, and we would pick new poems and new movements. We liked to do "crooked woman," "where the mississippi meets the amazon," "sue jean," and "third generation gechee men for your birthday," because the poems lent themselves to large movements that challenged the body and left the audience begging and yearning for more. We picked the poems to do sort of on a whim, but then we stuck with them until we felt comfortable with them, and we then turned to other poems to challenge ourselves to always be creative and not sink into the familiar. We rarely did the same program twice in a row, so our audience would not get bored. I learned to always do something fresh in San Francisco as I developed a following: always have one new thing.

I liked working with Mickey because she pulled from the words more meaning than I knew they had. She let me let the words sit on a movement as though they were being sung by a Marian Anderson or Harry Belafonte. Working with Mickey helped me learn to phrase the poems musically and choreographically so that there was a form to them that lent itself to the ear as opposed to the page. Eventually, Mickey began to choreograph whole pieces of mine such as *the love space demands* and other poem series. When Mickey worked, there was great emphasis put on physical strength. In order to do the movements, she wanted you to be in full control of your body and able to have the body do difficult things. So, the exercise she had for warm-ups required attention and great concentration on the power of muscle until exhaustion. But it always paid off in the end, and the movements always looked better, always looked easier. They were so strong until it looked like it couldn't possibly be hard.

> MICKEY DAVIDSON: I like talking about your characters in different situations other than the story line you wrote in the play. We did this a lot building up to the workshop performances of *Liliane* in Philadelphia [Freedom Theatre] and Rhode Island [Brown University]. There are two projects where you were the director and I the choreographer that stand out: The

project in LA with Billy Bang, violinist-composer, with an integrated cast of women; the piece took place in the basement of an abandoned church. And of course the twenty-fifth anniversary of *for colored girls* produced by Woodie King. It was important for you to put back a balance between acting and movement in revisiting what we call choreopoems. We developed a process of layering each other's work with the cast not being confused, and we blurred the lines between directing and choreographing. I enjoyed the process of creating *A Sense of Breath*, performed at the Whitney Museum with vocalist Jeanne Lee and Carline Ray on bass. It was truly a collaboration of women who, in the words of Cecil Taylor, "had good taste improvising." There was no director because we directed and edited ourselves.

These are things that stuck in my mind. I liked working with you, performing your own words, because the way you phrased your words and emotions was like hearing a musician playing music. You touched my core with an ease that made moving easy.

The love space demands is a choreopoem with eight players who also danced. There was a live band of six pieces and of course the eight players. The movements ranged from period African American dance to Afro-Cuban salsa and tango to portion inspired adagio. There was always the challenge of keeping balance because being off center was key to Davidson's choreography, so that one was always coming back to center after being off balance, but for a moment there was a question of whether or not we would come back to center and one was never certain. But you couldn't look like that. When choreographing for large pieces, Davidson liked to have three or four groups doing different things so that the movements pulled against each other and then came back together on one breath, as if a surprise. This happened during the opening of the poem "open up this is the police," when one half of the group was doing fast Latin steps and the other half was on the floor on their knees doing long prayerful-like leg stretches and sideways prayers. Arms outstretched, both groups would have different movement counts, one group fast and one group slow, but the arms would always be in sync. It was quite stunning to be a part of, and from the video I have seen, it was quite stunning to look at.

Mickey Davidson; the late Jeanne Lee, the chanteuse; and I performed at the Whitney Museum downtown in a piece we rehearsed in Philadelphia for over six months. In it, all three of us did dance solos, and all three of us sang. I wrote the poems, Jeanne improvised vocally, and Mickey danced. Mickey danced three solos, I did one, and we did several pieces as an ensemble. It was a very provocative and rousing experience. One of Mickey's solos was of a rape, which was wrenching and aching to watch. The power was in her legs and contractions. I had a chance to see Mickey work not only with Dianne at Sounds in Motion but also with Cecil Taylor the pianist. It was exciting to see her work with both McIntyre and Taylor. It required much of the same energy but in different ways. I worried that she would hurt herself dancing with Cecil Taylor because she would hurl herself through the air with such vehemence. While dancing with McIntyre, she found a delicacy and a buoyancy that eluded her that was not necessarily visible when dancing with Taylor. Both McIntyre and Taylor demanded different strength from Davidson, which she was able to deliver in full.

Davidson does not mirror the language of the poem. She extends, elaborates, anticipates, and responds to the words of the poem. To the sounds of the poem. Sometimes she throws a leg or puts a hip to the wind in such a way that the language punctuates the air more fully than I ordinarily would. Sometimes she jumps or grunts or smiles in such a way that the poem comes alive, in a new way, in a way that I had not planned. On her own, in silence, Davidson can seduce a word from me, propel an image out of my mouth, that is a secondary clause to her movement. In other words, Mickey's dance can create the space for language, so that the movement precedes the language and creates a space for words. For this experience, I am grateful for the power of Mickey Davidson's body, power, and thoughtfulness. Not unlike the early cave drawings in southern France, Mickey's visceral realities laid the groundwork for the development of the human soul so we can talk and walk.

HALIFU OSUMARE

T HE VILLAGE VANGUARD—a nightclub in New
York. On a muggy summer night, the Village
Vanguard was warm and crowded. The line
to see the legendary Pharoah Sanders, saxophonist, snaked
around the block. Seventh Avenue was abuzz with Black
people in dashikis and geles. I was sweating and tired from
dance class. But I was determined to get down the steps and
around the winding hall to the very dark space that looked
like a French café but was the Village Vanguard. A spot where
so many jazz musicians had honed their skills.

When I got in after showing my ID, there was only standing room, so I stood as close to the bandstand as was possible without offending someone. Pharoah picked up his horn,
and a booming tenor saxophone captivated the audience.
Leon Thomas, the vocalist, began "The Creator Has a Master Plan," and people's faces just lit up. The drummer, Nor-
man Connors, had everybody's feet moving. Then suddenly,
on the far-right elevated portion of the club, a young woman
with short cropped hair, thin of body and long of legs, began

to dance. The loose clothing she had on floated through the air as her arms swept across the sitting patrons. She was so vibrant and innovative, demonstrating West African, Cuban, and what seemed like Haitian movement and fabulous improvisation. Everyone's gaze bounced between Pharoah and this dancer who was attracting so much attention, yet her actions did not distract from the music; they amplified it. They made the human body part of the band. She was golden and glistening as the night went on, and she danced until the music ended. She got as much applause as the band. And she hugged Pharoah when he put his horn down. They had made a fabulous ensemble.

HALIFU OSUMARE: As a dancer I've been known as a dance improviser. I like to improvise, and I have taught dance improvisation in formal classes. Remember that story you keep telling about the first time you met me dancing at the Village Vanguard, improvising to Pharoah Sanders's music? If I felt the spirit of a particular kind of music, especially if it was live music, I was known to jump up and start dancing. Just go for it. So, I became known to musicians as someone who could really hold her own with them, especially jazz musicians. I can get in there and add the movement component to their improvisation and create a dialogue. I often approach my choreography by just starting to improvise, starting at a place and finding phrases that really make sense to me, that I can use to realize the piece and make connections, particularly to African Americans.

There was a sign on the window in San Francisco's Fillmore District that a series of Haitian dance classes could begin in a week. No one before this had offered Haitian dance, only Afro-Cuban and Brazilian had been available before. So, I was excited. I signed up and put my money down for the series and secured a space. The day I walked into the studio I situated myself in the middle third row, back to the right of where the teacher would be so that I could see every movement. I realized that the woman who was about to lead the class was the same woman I had seen dancing in New York at the Village Vanguard. There was no possibility that she would remember me because I was just part of a huge crowd of admirers, but I certainly remembered her. Class began in an unusual way for me because we started to dance immediately. At first, there were small steps one side to the other. And it became more complicated as knees were bent and bodies contracted, adding to the pulsing of the feet. Next, the arms were added, and you bent the head while it circled around. Eventually, even the fingers and wrists would be involved in the series.

HALIFU OSUMARE: My main influence is Katherine Dunham. She influenced my dance career and my approach to dance and life itself, because she always said that Dunham technique is a way of life, and that's the way I teach it as a certified Dunham instructor. Miss Dunham set the model for me as an artist-scholar—that being an artist did not preclude you from being a researcher, scholar, and a writer. I have followed suit with that particular approach to my dance career. Besides Katherine Dunham, I would say in my early days it was Ed Mock, like with you. He was a very important influence in my early days in terms of giving me a sense of the freedom to explore my own movement.

NTOZAKE SHANGE: What was it about the Dunham
philosophy that attracted you?

HO: That it was wholistic. That it showed the integration of mind, body, and spirit, and that the dancer had
to develop all three. And she continued to develop her
technique, teaching us how to start the dance class
with breathing exercises that helped the student to
center him- or herself, bringing them into the present moment, which is so crucial to them dancing
effectively. That wholistic approach included a direct
connection with the spirit and the body, along with
her theories on form and function, intercultural com-
munication, and socialization through the arts, which
emphasized that the arts are one of the main socialization tools within many cultures, and it definitely is on
the African continent. This continued into the Americas, concerning socializing the individual from birth
to death through dance and music. So those kinds of
approaches to dance, which went beyond just learning
steps or routines, were very influential, and I think it is
one of Ms. Dunham's main contributions.

NS: You know what that reminds me of? It reminds me
of when I couldn't speak more than one language. And
when I traveled around the Americas, as long as I could
keep up conversationally with the culture of that country, I was accepted.

HO: Right, that's what held me in good stead as well.
As I traveled, I would try to learn some of the language
to be able to communicate, but the moment I started

dancing, that would be the instant communicator. And I could connect with people anywhere in the world— Europe, South America, the Caribbean, you know anywhere. It was the language of body and spirit.

Finally, I realized that although I had expected simple exercises and a warm-up, we had just done that, even though it felt like we were actually dancing. This was Halifu Osumare's typical beginning, so that every movement strengthened the body. And every movement carved a form in the air. She explained to us that because Caribbean people lived on islands, their movements reflected the softness of the waves receding from the soil, the strength of the waves approaching, but always there was a softness, no jagged, jerky, or angular hard edges, especially in Haitian dance. She found the rippling of the spine to engender the resilience of the Haitian people and believed that dance was revealing of the politics of a place as a propagandist.

HALIFU OSUMARE: A lot of people don't understand that dance is a total integration of the mind, body, and spirit. When you truly dance, that's what you're doing. It's not just learning some steps or routines really well; it is about finding a way to integrate your mind and your spirit with your body as you express yourself. And the other concept, for me, about dance is that it's visualized text. People don't think of dance as text, because they are thinking about the written word. I'm a writer and I understand the two medias, but dance is like a text to me. It's just like written word, and I think that as we grow as a society, we have to become more literate in being able to read the body.

I was exhausted when the class was over and was responding to muscles in my back that I didn't know I had. It was hard to move from Dunham, Mock, and Sawyer to the soft curves and slippery hips of my new teacher's repertoire. I was impressed. The next day before class, I presented her with the deepest red apple I could find and went back to my space.

> HALIFU OSUMARE: I began to discover Black history through researching the dances in different eras of our history, from the plantation era to contemporary times. I found a special connection to myself as a Black person and as a Black artist, as well as the larger history of our people and how that can be illuminated through theater, dance, and music. So, I've always been about that. I say at the very end of my memoir, *Dancing in Blackness*, that part of what I've been doing all my life is receiving ancestral messages and translating them in my art.

At Everybody's Dance Studio, Halifu began to teach a class on a regular basis. It ranged from African dance to jazz. I went at every opportunity to soak up new movements I was discovering. Eventually, Halifu asked me to join her company, along with Elvia Marta and Aisha Kahlil, to do a production of hers called *The Evolution of Black Dance*, which traced the history of African American movement from Africa to the present day. Beginning with movements from Ghana, we went through ring shouts, spear dances, clogging, the cakewalk, Charleston, jitterbug, and boogie-woogie. Any movement a Black person did was traced through this hour-long production. Halifu had us perform in schools and YMCAs all over the Bay Area. It was challenging to get ready to be on stage at 10 a.m., but we did it, and she had engagements. She would pick us up individually because none of us had cars. I made the mistake of turning off my phone because I didn't want to be bothered and was roundly scolded by Halifu who said that it was very unprofessional to be unreachable, and she would not stand for it. The next project Halifu had was *Four Women: Images of the Black Woman in Monologue, Song, and Dance*, in which four women performed monologues of Black women in music, sound, and dance. I played a bag woman and was so good until one performance when I tried to make my entrance from outside. The usher would not let me enter the theater. She threatened to call the police if I didn't stop banging on the door. Finally, she opened the door to say she would call the police. I said, "Not until I make my entrance," whereupon she got out of my way, and I entered late but loudly.

NTOZAKE SHANGE: When did you realize that you had to dance?

HALIFU OSUMARE: I guess it was when I made the transition from high school to undergraduate school at San Francisco State. I couldn't bring myself to major in dance, but I kept wanting to take dance classes because I had started in high school, and I realized it could be a profession. I had seen films of a professional dance company, and I was just so drawn to it. My parents didn't want me to major in dance, so I minored in it.

Also, I think it was a dance class that I was taking with Ed Mock. He was teaching some kind of Afro-Cuban dance with drumming, and before that class I had only danced to a pianist who played either contemporary music or classical European music. When I heard those drums, it was hard for me to really keep up with the rhythm. Ed used to always scream at me, saying, "Get on the beat, Janis," which was my name at the time. "Can't you hear it?" I kept working harder, and it was finally during one of his classes what I call an inner cultural ear opened up. Once I really could hear and identify with those rhythms, I was never the same again. I think when I began to move to the drums, that's what really made me know that I had to dance. It was something that I could no longer ignore, no matter what my parents said; I had to follow the dance. It was like the beat of the drums called me and that was it. I knew I had to do it, no matter what. That really reinforced a kind of self-empowerment in me: to follow my own voice and not listen to others.

My experience with Halifu has not only taught me about the discipline of being a professional dancer, but it also taught me about the joy. I will never forget she reminded me that Bernice Ross, a San Francisco–based dancer-choreographer had refused to hire me because I was late for rehearsal because my water was turned off and I had to see to it. Halifu said, "You've got to keep your water and your phone on because you got to be able to take care of yourself or you can't dance for me." I never made those mistakes again.

HALIFU OSUMARE: Being able to improvise to your poetry was another phase in my dance career and my artistic development as a dancer. Before that I had only been working with music, and your poetry to me represented a kind of music, with the way you wrote and the rhythm you used in your poetry. So, it was easy to improvise at the readings that we did together because of the way you wrote, and your relationship to words. I just felt connected because your words were musical, and it was easy for me. I really developed as an artist by working with you, and of course that made me understand and embody all our work together. We informed each other.

Learning the movements of West Africa and eastern New York, Texas, and Los Angeles melded the experiences of Black people in dance for me. I was lucky that Halifu had experienced all these things and could instill that aesthetic in me. She was a combination of the twentieth century and sixteenth-century African art. What a blessing! I shall never forget the ring shouts that Aisha did, and we got so happy we thought we were in church. That's what dancing with Halifu could do for you.

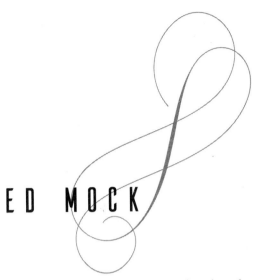

ED MOCK

I N THE DAYS OF AFROS, before braids and locks were popular, it was strange to see a young man with a bald head. But Ed Mock was resolute as he walked down and about the San Francisco streets. West Coast Dance Works was located in the downtown industrial area of San Francisco. I could tell I was approaching the wide-open space where we worked because there would be at least four long-haul trucks poking out into the streets near the door. Up one flight of stairs and a right turn and you were bowled over by the light.

Light in the Bay Area is crystalline, unlike that of the light back east, where you see the air has been breathed before. Young women and a few fellows would gather together in the dressing room to get ready for class. This was a different group of people from the population of Raymond Sawyer's company or Halifu Osumare's company. Here white jazz dancers and dancers on hiatus from the Las Vegas chorus lines wanting to stay in touch with the muscles and rhythm worked with Ed Mock, whose every move seemed to be choreographed by the jazz gods on high. There was a discipline to the class that Ed seemed to expect just by his posture and his silence. As he clapped his hands in a 4/4 rhythm, he demonstrated the movement with an eye on all of us.

Ed believed in partnering, so all our exercises were done with someone else. I had a kind female partner and we would switch off. First my stretches came, then her stretches, then my lifts, then her leg lifts. It all seemed to be in defiance of gravity. We were constantly pressing our feet against one another or pulling our arms away or to one another in second-position wide pliés. We felt the jazz port de bras laying down flat as well as sitting upright. We'd repeat the same in fourth-position plié and again in first. Jazz pirouettes were more difficult for me to handle than the turned-out ballet pirouettes, but I hung in there. All I could do was fall, which I did.

Once I was ahead of the line doing across-the-floor exercises with Marcia Blanck, another transplanted Easterner. We were to do grand jeté leaps across the floor, just as Ed had done, as blithely as a butterfly. Marcia and I looked at each other, smiled, put our arms in second position, and leapt. I felt my foot come off the ground and I knew I was flying and then thud. The next thing I knew I looked over and Marcia was sitting on the floor staring at me. We had fallen on the count of two. There was nothing we could do but laugh and go to the end of the line.

Ed did not seem too perturbed by our failure, and the whole class laughed at us.

Ed choreographed and did exercises to contemporary pop music and rhythm and blues. Always upbeat and demanding or singularly heartfelt. A joy in the movement that secured sadness or torture with its beauty. There was this duality in

Ed's work that suggested jocularity but was always fraught with the tension of the people, the lovers, and the solitary.

What was more important, Ed encouraged us to create our own dances, not improvisation but full-out dances that didn't necessarily require movements but did need to present a complete aesthetic statement. I am sure that's one of the reasons I had the temerity to create *for colored girls*—one of the first solos I choreographed for Ed's class became the frenzied staccato movement that we first see in "somebody/anybody sing a Black girl's song."

Interestingly enough, when I performed this dance to Roscoe Mitchell's *Nonaah*, Ed put on a sinister-looking worn black overcoat, a broad-rimmed black hat, and dark glasses and stood behind me doing slow intimidating movements as the title of the play, "and this is *for colored girls who have considered suicide/when the rainbow is enuf*, lights out," could be heard from the recording. He scared me to death, but later, at the party we had, he told me to keep that movement because I was on to something. He reminded me that if there was anything he could do to help, just let him know. He said there was more to come; I just had to find it. I took him up on that.

The first performance of the show was done at West Coast Dance Works, rent free, lights and sound complimentary. Ed nurtured the dream Paula Moss and I had at the very beginnings of our grand adventure.

AN INTERVIEW WITH

DYANE HARVEY

NTOZAKE SHANGE: Dyane, who do you consider to be your mentors?

DYANE HARVEY: I consider that every choreographer that I have worked intimately with served as a mentor, in that they have had a profound effect on my growth as an artist, how I express myself as a human being. People who have nurtured my development substantially are my first serious ballet teacher from Schenectady, New York, Marilyn Ramsey—if she hadn't given me those scholarships year after year, who knows what I would have become?—Paul Sanasardo helped me balance my diet of ballet training to begin processing his form—a combination of Graham and ballet—and eventually join the ranks of "modern dancers" in the early '70s. Others include Eleo Pomare, Ron Pratt, John Parks, Dianne McIntyre, Joan Miller, Fred Benjamin, Abdel Salaam—my husband, Otis Sallid, Chuck Davis, Shawneequa Baker-Scott, Diana Ramos, and George Faison.

Alvin Ailey was never a mentor, but his work did have a profound effect on my life when I was a member of the Alvin Ailey Repertory Company.

NS: Was your training through a university or in the studio?

DH: All of my training has been in "the studio." I told my mother, to her horror, that I wanted to learn dance while doing it, not studying at it. So I left home, was given an extended scholarship with Paul Sanasardo at his school, Modern Dance Artists, and I began my New York training, augmented at the Clark Center [for the Performing Arts] with Thelma Hill, James Truitte, and Rod Rodgers. Later on, I studied with Eleo Pomare at his studio and at the first Ailey school, at the Firehouse on Fifty-Ninth Street.

NS: Do you have your own company or are you a part of one?

DH: I am a founding member of Forces of Nature Dance Theatre and, since 1981, have had the honor and joy of assisting in the growth of our repertory. At this time, I have no desire to choreograph for a professional company, unless commissioned to participate in a special project. The experiences I enjoy the most are the processes when working with actors on plays/dramas that require movement.

NS: Is teaching a part of your work?

DH: I do teach, at Hofstra University, Lehman College, and at Princeton University. It pays the bills and challenges my creativity. The course I teach at Princeton is devoted to examining the contributions of traditional and contemporary African and African American dance forms to the culture of the USA. Courses at the other schools are titled simply Modern Dance. I am free to teach basically what I choose, and I have chosen to place a heavy emphasis on the effects of African American movement forms on American modern dance.

NS: Do you use live music or recordings?

DH: When I teach, I am blessed to have an accompanist, and in some instances I have choreographed and performed works using live music. The pieces that my husband choreographs in the traditional African form are always done to live drumming. This was a curiously frustrating experience for me at first, learning to listen to a drum orchestra and move within the rhythms. Financially it is a challenge; you must prepare a budget that is large enough to cover the expense of a single live musician or group of live musicians. So, the second-best choice is recorded sound. Even here the most interesting aspect is to have music composed for the movement, which is still a part of that wonderful sharing of creative energies.

NS: How do you integrate Black experiences into your work? Do you think it's important to incorporate Black vernacular dance into choreography?

DH: When I am assigned a project that specifies work in the vernacular, I use the forms as freely as possible. Years ago, I was embarrassed by Hollywood's images of Black people and decided to give myself therapy. I went to the Lincoln Center library and researched plantation and early minstrel dances, and finally learned to accept and embrace the form and history that accompanied the movements. When choreographing for *The African Company Presents Richard III*, I used different forms of period dancing—including plantation. Although I am not a tapper, I am sensitive to honoring the journey of rhythm throughout the body and allowing for its full expression during performance or a lesson. Embracing these particular "takes" on vernacular dance expression has helped me to heal parts of a wounded psyche and has given me much more physical information to pull from.

NS: Is there a piece that you consider to be your signature?

DH: As a performer first, I feel that my signature piece is *Roots*, choreographed by Eleo Pomare. When I performed it at Syvilla Fort's tribute on Broadway at the Majestic Theatre—then the home of *The Wiz*; I had just gotten the job as a swing a week prior—during the tribute . . . I felt I became larger than myself.

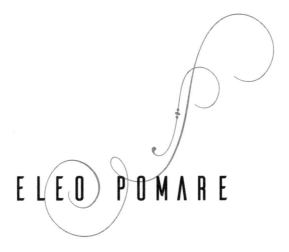

E L E O   P O M A R E

ON THE FIRST DAY I saw Eleo Pomare I had just
finished a raucous class with Raymond Sawyer: heart palpitating, adrenaline rushing, and
sweat pouring. I finally got home, prepared a steaming hot
bath with bubbles, brewed a pot of fresh Ethiopian coffee,
and proceeded to take my bath. I fell asleep, and a strange
smell awakened me. I rushed to the kitchen to find there was
a hole in the bottom of the coffeepot. I had been so exhausted
that I slept through a perking pot of coffee and the demise of
the coffeepot. There was barely time to dress in my finery and
get ready to see Pomare. I jumped into a pair of worn jeans, a
sequined top, a leather jacket, and a black beret. Off I went to
the San Francisco Civic Center to see the fabled Eleo Pomare.

The theater was hushed when I got there. The audience
was anxious, so I knew I hadn't missed anything. There was
a flash of light emanating from the stage. The roar of a high-
speed motorcycle accompanied by six dancers to one side.
Finally, when the light came up on the motorcycle, there was

Pomare himself, dark brown, wiry, and petite. He straddled the bike. When he rose, he contracted and leapt into a frenzy of attitude jetés. They were so ferocious, until I thought he was just over my head.

> ELEO POMARE: I teach classes for individual dance companies, at conferences, and at universities when invited. But my greatest joy is teaching high school students, whose minds and bodies are most eager to learn. I feel that it is with the younger people that I have the greatest impact. Performances resulting from my teaching experiences with teenagers are proof to me that this is a most worthwhile effort.

> NTOZAKE SHANGE: How heavily is your work influenced by Western traditional form, classical, and modern dance? Do you integrate any other cultures into your work? Indigenous, African, Caribbean, or other cultural dances?

> EP: I have been influenced by all of the forms you name. You will see, subtly and sometimes not so subtly, a blend of two or more of those forms in much, if not most, of my work. Notably, I am currently remounting a work, *Back to Bach*, which may look to most like a blend of ballet and modem, but the discerning—most white critics won't notice—will notice distinctive Watusi movements interwoven throughout. This is a contribution to American dance that you won't find most white choreographers making.

The next time I saw him I was in his class in New York on the sixth floor [in a building] on Sixteenth Street. As I was lying on the floor, I tried my best to lift my legs and keep my back flat, letting my legs down one at a time until they were four inches off the floor, then the other leg. I think I turned purple from trying to keep my breath even. Suddenly I heard Pomare with his drum over my head, beating the drum, watching me intently. It was strange that my eyes were open because usually when I was trying to do the exercises they were closed.

"Ms. Shange, what are you thinking about? Are you thinking about your legs?"

I looked at him blankly, nodding.

"I think you are thinking about something else besides dance." Blankly I nodded again. "Well, if it is not dance, what are you thinking about?"

I looked at him directly, legs still in the air. "I am thinking about a poem."

"Well for God's sake, go home and write. When you are here, think about dance or don't come."

Totally abashed, I scurried like a little mouse to get my things and go to my safe typewriter, where I was in control.

ELEO POMARE: I feel that the arts are all interconnected or intertwined. I paint. I write poetry and prose. I design costumes. I admire the work of others who compose music and those who create sculptures.

NTOZAKE SHANGE: When did you realize that you had to choreograph?

EP: I always knew I wanted to be a performing artist. When I saw little opportunity for a small-framed Black male in acting, which was my first choice, I turned to choreography and my best means of expressing myself. It stuck.

NS: Is there anyone you've looked to throughout your career as a mentor?

EP: My role model was and is James Baldwin and his body of work. His writings have had the greatest impact on me. Studying dance composition with Louis Horst has had the most direct impact on my approach to choreography.

NS: Did you have university or studio training?

EP: Because I felt that university training would interfere with my creative psyche, I turned initially to the José Limón studio as a place where the artistic style was of the most interest to me. Later, I studied with Kurt Jooss in Germany. His *Green Table* was a primary inspiration for me to go on choreographing.

After several more episodes of Pomare's drum and his constant chastening I got used to taking the class. In fact, my whole body seemed to change; it became more muscular and lean. I was proud of the way I looked. I felt myself start to smile; then I realized that I better keep track of the time. I had an appointment with Dr. Pineda, my OB-GYN. Hoping I would not cause too much of a ruckus, I tried to slip out of the studio.

"Ms. Shange, are you going somewhere?"

I turned and nodded my head. "Yes, I have an appointment."

"Then by all means, keep your appointment," he said, and I was quickly out the door.

My pelvis still throbbed from all the abdominal exercises

we had done. I thought people could see my tummy going up down up as I walked across the street to the subway. By the time I got to the doctor, I was spent. On the exam table, legs astride in the stirrups, Dr. Pineda said, "Well, Ms. Shange, you've really done it this time," and I braced myself to hear what contagious disease I had contracted. "You're pregnant, my dear."

Pregnant?—as if not understanding what happens when you join a man and woman.

"Yes indeed," Dr. Pineda said, with a small smile. "We've got to get ready for the big event. I'll see you in three weeks."

From then on, I've always associated Eleo with the birth of my daughter, Savannah. After all, my stomach was contracting all the way from class to the office. That had to be the baby.

NTOZAKE SHANGE: Do you involve yourself in movement with antebellum African American dance, minstrels, tap, vernacular dance—swing, Creole quadrilles?

ELEO POMARE: I have drawn inspiration from all of the above forms. In one work, *Over Here*, I depict a tap-dancing minstrel dangling from the end of a noose. That might give you an idea of how I orchestrate ideas and dance forms.

NS: Why is this important to you?

EP: These *forms* are important as springboards for exploration beyond the narrow scope of European movement.

NS: Is there a piece of work that you consider to be your signature or representative of your style?

EP: I don't think about my work that way. There is no single work that "defines" me or that "signifies" me, is my "signature" as an artist. I *have* to choreograph every work that I do. The works are varied, some serious, some whimsical, some political, some just fun, some educational, some angry, and some celebratory. As a body, my work is my signature.

The last time I saw Eleo we watched a video of his *The House of Bernarda Alba*. The slow legato of the movement foreshadowed his impending death. At least the last time I saw him I was watching something he was really proud of.

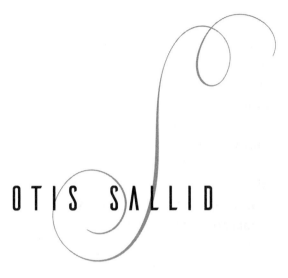

OTIS SALLID

WHEN YOU SEE OTIS SALLID DANCE, you can smell a man. I first saw Otis at Roger Furman's New Heritage Repertory Theatre. After a production of *On Strivers Row*, with the indomitable Laurie Carlos, I was still sweating from class with Dianne McIntyre down on 125th Street in Harlem, but the rumors about *Strivers Row* had been so intense and long-lasting that I had to see it, sweat or no sweat. I spotted Sallid across the house thoroughly enjoying himself, so that the lines of the play seemed to rivet his body. The next time I saw Otis Sallid was at a Black dance conference in New York. The hotel was abuzz with African American and African dancers from around the world.

OTIS SALLID: I have been very fortunate to have many great mentors in my life. Usually, people only get one, but I have had several. These people have taken the time and made a difference in my life and my artistic development.

Shawneequa Baker-Scott was a mentor to me

because she was my very first teacher at the Kennedy Center in Harlem. She allowed me to be a boy amongst a sea of girls and taught me how to stand on my own in a room and on the stage. She was married to a boxer named Scotty. He taught me how to box, but that only lasted until I was punched in the face.

Thelma Hill was a mentor to me because she taught me how to dance. We were close, as she took a liking to me and made sure I was on the straight and narrow. Ms. Hill made me clear about the power of Black dance and its relationship to the Horton technique. She taught me about dancing with clarity and cleanliness. She also taught me respect for the craft. Showing up on time, making sure your tights were clean and not with a lot of holes in them. I could not afford tights back then, so this was a bit of a struggle. But I made it work. Respect for the craft.

Eleo Pomare I consider a dance mentor because he taught me how to tell stories. He taught me the importance of digging deeper into the second and third skin of a subject. There was always a need to find the core and central idea of a story and to express it in ways that illuminate the ideas in that story. He taught me to tell the little story.

Debbie Allen I consider a mentor because she taught me how to choreograph and direct for the camera. It is a completely different discipline than choreographing for the theater. I learned from her how to get your choreography onto the screen and how to get what you think of your choreography onto the screen as well. She would say to me, "Don't show the camera what you

Halifu Osumare, Aisha Kahlil, and Ntozake Shange dancing in Oakland, California, circ. 1970s.

Katherine Dunham, the "Matriarch of Black Dance," in *Tropical Revue* (1943), at New York's Martin Beck Theatre.

Performance of *it has not always been this way*, by Ntozake Shange and Dianne McIntyre's Sounds in Motion dance company at Symphony Space, New York, NY, June 1981. Poetry by Ntozake Shange, choreography by Dianne McIntyre, sets by Candace Hill Montgomery, costumes by Terri Cousar Shockley, and music by Amina Claudine Myers. Pictured: Ntozake Shange (center) with Cheryl Banks-Smith, Sheila Barker, Jacquelyn Bird, Mickey Davidson, and Dianne McIntyre.

In this photo from *it has not always been this way*, pictured (left to right) are Dianne McIntyre, Ntozake Shange, Sheila Barker, and Cheryl Banks-Smith.

Ntozake Shange in 1977.

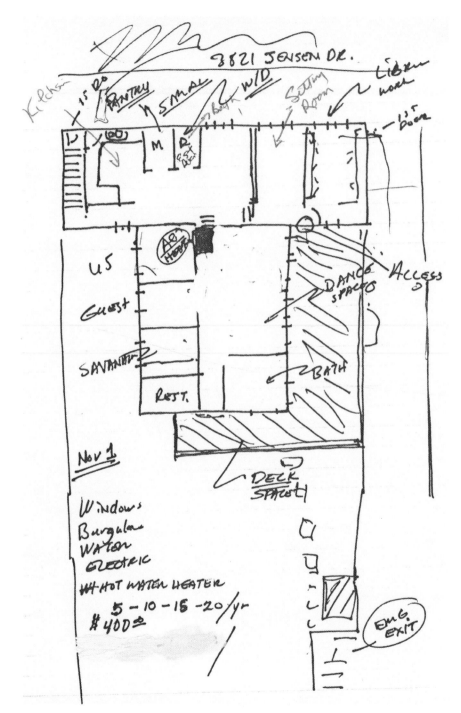

Sketches by Ntozake of the floor plan for her house at 3821 Jensen Drive.

Ntozake Shange and the dancer and choreographer Dianne McIntyre.

Ntozake with a cast of *for colored girls who have considered suicide/when the rainbow is enuf.*

A young Ntozake Shange in the late 1970s.

Ntozake Shange at the Reid Lecture, Women Issues
Luncheon, at Barnard College Women's Center, in
November 1978.

Ntozake posing in 1981.

Ntozake Shange with Concert Ensemble: (left to right) Malachi Favors, Lester Bowie, Kahil El'Zabar, and Hamiet Bluiett, circa 1980s.

These three photos are from the 2019 production of *for colored girls who have considered suicide/when the rainbow is enuf* at the Public Theater in New York, directed by Leah C. Gardiner and choreographed by Camille A. Brown.

don't want it to see." Though simple this was profound. She also taught me how to run a film set as a choreographer and a director.

And Martha Graham, I had the fortune of studying with and attending her school. She was an amazing theoretician. She had a million theories, concepts, and ideas about the dance. There was something sacred about her work. Martha Graham was a mentor because she taught me that nothing mattered but the dance itself. Also, a great dance can make a change in the world. It also is an equalizer. It makes us all one.

There was no way to escape the frenetic energy of these performers, but I escaped to chat with Hector Lino, the Black Guatemalan cultural essayist. We reviewed and critiqued dancers we hadn't seen and the politics of Black dance companies and their members. We must have been pretty raucous because all of sudden the door flew open and there was none other than Otis Sallid in the portal, muscular, Black, and gleaming with a smile so broad you'd think he had seen Santa Claus. What was stunning was his approach to me. "Ntozake, where have you been?" I didn't have a chance to answer before he literally swept me off my feet into his arms, and he bid Hector farewell.

NTOZAKE SHANGE: Do you have a company of your own?

OTIS SALLID: No, I do not have a company, though many times I wish I did. In the 1980s I put a company together called the New Art Ensemble. In our first sea-

son, I produced the dance company on Broadway at
the Edison Theatre. Gregory Hines gave me the money
to make it happen. It was great. Debbie Allen, Michael
Peters, Hinton Battle, Dyane Harvey, Ben Harney, Shir-
ley Black-Brown, Michael DeLorenzo were all a part of
that company. They were all young, beautiful, talented,
and all different. But soon thereafter Hollywood called
and we went running.

NS: Do you teach?

OS: I teach whenever I get a chance and wherever I go,
especially in small towns that could use someone like
myself. I'll take the time and seek out the local school in
the town where I am producing a project and teach for
free or for whatever they can afford to pay. Much like
the many people who have mentored me, I pay it forward. I pay it forward.

I think that I have taught in almost every state in the
country. I learned to do that from Langston Hughes.
There is a need to preserve the Black dance tradition,
which is most powerful and creative. I try to pass it on.

There was a time in the late '60s when Black dance
was a power to be reckoned with. This time in Black
historical dance has never been preserved or collected.
No one knows about it. So, I teach about it as much as
possible.

Female dancers are always gossiping about the men who lift
us in the middle of a piece and how well they can control our
bodies or how well they support us as we glide in the air, six
feet off the ground. Does he have a firm grip on my back? Are

my legs OK? Will he let me go without warning? Am I safe? These are the questions we ask as we lift our bodies and focus our energy on our pelvic muscles, so we are in good form as we are poised in the air. Otis Sallid held me as if I was as light as a feather. I could feel the strength in his arm and back as he carried me down the hallways past plain hotel rooms with numbers that seemed to race as we moved.

NTOZAKE SHANGE: How does your work relate to the African American experience?

OTIS SALLID: Funny that you should ask that, because it is always related to the African American experience. Simply by the mere fact that I am an African American. It is my story and my ancestral blood memory that is interwoven into the very fabric of my work. It never sleeps. It is always with me. It is never about steps. Steps are tertiary. It is always about the spirit. My spirit is the African American spirit.

NS: Are you more drawn to dance or choreographing?

OS: I am not sure how to answer that. I don't see dance and choreography in terms of steps anymore. I see it in language, thoughts, and expressions of ideas. Do the audience and artists participating understand what the work is saying?

For me, everything influences my work as a cho-reographer. Broadway, Off-Broadway, concert dance, cabaret, music videos, commercials. All things are influ-enced by everything. There are no lines anymore.

Let me say this about my process. I enter into each

situation with a clean slate. I am not afraid to not know what I am about to do. I trust the spirit and I trust what I know. Then there is a moment before you begin to choreograph when the blood rushes to the memory and you are filled with all the things known and unknown. The presence of God is upon you. It asks you, "Why are you doing this? Why is this important to you? Why are you here?" You ask it, "Why are you in front of me? Why have you appeared?" It has placed itself in front of your life. And at that moment, if it is right for you, the spirit descends. This is a sacred place and moment.

Once all things are confirmed, you are lifted up and out of your body to a place that allows you to move through your work with ease. This place is your arsenal of remembrance. It is your inspiration. It is your muse working through you.

I thought of the characters in a Frank Yerby novel, the Black writer who traced the antebellum South and the treatment of enslaved Americans in the South. The male characters were always muscular and defiant. I thought of their women and children buffeted from the ship to the shore crying or screaming, "Never, never, never," in whatever language they spoke. In one novel a woman grabbed her infant child and ran with her to the cliff overlooking the ocean to avoid her fate. She stood for a moment on the edge—infant in her arms—and looked back to see a robust Black man running toward her with arms outstretched just before she jumped. The look on the man's face when he turned to see the overseer coming after him was so full of rebelliousness that you feared for his life.

That is how it feels to be carried by Otis Sallid down a hallway. You are saved from the possibility of falling. Sallid's grasp on my thigh and between my shoulder blades assured my safety and the line of beauty his movement compelled. This is one of the elements you encounter when you dance with Otis Sallid. Along with lyricism, strength, and good form, Sallid offers the opportunity for a dancer's body that we dream of.

AN INTERVIEW WITH

CAMILLE A. BROWN

NTOZAKE SHANGE: Who do you consider to be among your mentors and why?

CAMILLE A. BROWN: Dianne McIntyre and Marlies Yearby. Both of them are inspiring, intellectual, heartfelt, honest, and I always learn so much from them in terms of navigating a career in both concert dance and theater. Seeing them working in the field is astonishing to me, especially being a Black female, knowing racism and sexism are still very present in our society. Their presence helps me to stay on task in a very special and focused way.

NS: Were they of assistance to you technically? In terms of your technique?

CB: Absolutely. Their openness and willingness to bring other voices into the room. Their vulnerability, intellect, and rigor. All lessons. In terms of my dance upbringing, I'm originally from Jamaica, Queens, New York, and started my dance training at Bernice Johnson's Cultural Arts Center when I was four. I also went to Carolyn DeVore [Dance Center], then to LaGuardia High School, and received my BFA from [the University of] North Carolina School of the Arts. After college, I danced with Ronald K. Brown's Evidence dance company for five seasons before focusing on my choreographic voice full time. That's my trajectory.

NS: You do have a company of your own?

CB: Yes.

NS: When you were deciding to form your own company, what was your vision?

CB: At first, I didn't want to have my own company.

NS: Why not?

CB: Because when I was in Evidence, all the extra work Ron had to do—on top of being the artistic director—seemed very intimidating to me. He wasn't just a choreographer; he was a manager, he had to go to this meeting and that meeting. It seemed like he never was able to have a little peace, and I just didn't know if I had the stamina to take that on. I also didn't think I was capable of creating a language that was all my own and that said something—anything. I was not in the headspace to understand the power of having your own voice. It wasn't until I started choreographing for other companies that I realized the need [for] and importance of my own troupe. I wanted to have a more intimate working relationship with people and make space to figure out what my voice was. It wasn't going to happen with companies I would be spending only two or three weeks with. That kind of investigation would need to be with people I trusted. It's been the best decision of my life. My company is my family. There's nothing like walking into a space and having no idea what you are going to do, but knowing no matter what, no one will judge you. My company has my back, and there's nothing like that feeling.

NS: When you were selecting dancers, was it harder to select men or women?

CB: At first, I was just looking for people who had the ability to do character work. From there, I realized a specificity was needed when describing the kind of dancer I wanted in the room. The more time I had to figure it out, I got better at understanding what my voice was. My dancers needed to be exceptionally gifted at character and improvisational work alongside a keen understanding of all movement genres. The two of these together made the search harder. When you find those people you're like, "Aah, this is wonderful," and you begin to assess that every dancer is not conditioned to dissect something as an actor does. And that's how I treat my dancers—as actors. It wasn't a question of

more men or women; it was a question of who can
do the work.

NS: Are you willing to share your process?

CB: My process, yeah. It's challenging because with
every piece, I try to create a new language. Not a new
language in the sense that it looks like a different choreographer, but a different language for that specific work.
So, if you have five pieces, each one should be distinct.
I hope the audience will identify a piece with that language and world. At the beginning of every process, I
try to strip myself down and re-inform. Over the years,
I have come to accept my process. At first I felt because
I was different, it was wrong. But I have learned to love
my process. It's scary because I am always trying to
challenge myself and make room for discoveries in real
time, and to trust my instincts has been something I'm
continuously working on. We are building and creating together. We're all taking the dive. This is why the
choices of the dancers and the musicians are crucial to
the work. Creative and brave energy is a must. Just like
a director asks actors to investigate, I ask my company
to do the same. It takes time and it can be tedious and
frustrating, but in the end, it's very fulfilling. My process for developing a work takes one to two years. It's
one of the main reasons I pulled back from creating
works for other companies. For me, two to three weeks
of rehearsal is one good four-count-of-eight-phrase. I
like having the time to figure things out. Be in process.
It's what I love about theater. Even though it feels jam

packed, and everything must be complete in a very
short amount of time, the years it takes to build one
show is something very special and important. Concert
dance and theater are different, but I am deeply inspired
by the process time required for the latter.

NS: This next question, I'm going to ask it a couple of
different ways. Your work is directly connected to the
African American experience, right?

CB: Yes.

NS: OK, elaborate.

CB: Well, it's the African American experience through
my eyes and my collaborators', musicians', and dancers'.
It's really easy to fall into generalizing how Black people
live, so I am specific when saying it's my perspective
and experiences. For instance, *Black Girl: Linguistic
Play* is not about *the* Black girl, but it is *a* Black girl's
story. It follows the maturation of a Black girl into a
woman, and is told in three sections. three duets. *BG:
LP* is about sisterhood, friendship, and how there may
be conflict at times but we never let each other go. We
hold onto sisterhood. It's about mothers and daughters
and the nuance of that relationship. [The dance] *ink*,
which I choreographed in 2017, connects the gestural
information of the African tradition with the movement
and gestural language of the African American experience. There is a lineage of choreographers who have
explored the African/African American experience:

Dianne McIntyre, Marlies Yearby, Jawole Willa Jo Zollar, Ronald K. Brown, Rennie Harris, Kyle Abraham, Bill T. Jones, and many others. We're all talking about the experiences of Black people but in our own ways—as we should—because our stories are dimensional.

NS: OK, that's a good one. That's a good way to start. When did you know you had to dance, you had to choreograph?

CB: I knew I had to dance when that's all I had. I felt it was all I had. I got teased *a lot* when I was younger. My voice was always considered "strange," "high," and "weird." It was extremely hurtful and also made me very insecure. My voice never really changed, so I had to work to love it. It's gotten a little deeper, but people still know when I'm down the hall lol. Movement was a way for me to create a safe space for myself. I didn't have to worry about being teased. It was home. I would observe people in conversation and think how easy it seemed for them. For me, it was like moving a mountain. When I move, it's my greatest expression. I was led to choreography by way of rejection. During my dance training, some teachers—not all—made it clear I did not have "the ideal body" or look of a dancer.

NS: So the balancing thing really got to you?

CB: The weight issues got to me. People assume this is just an issue in the ballet world, but it happens in modern too. Some teachers made me feel like I just wasn't "it." It's hard to describe. Many teachers were supportive of my dance education, but you also remember teachers at the opposite end of the spectrum. I was dismissed and it was tough. People look at me crazy when I talk of my experiences. To be young and still growing but told you're overweight is very confusing. I was sent to the nutritionist every year. This was my norm.

NS: Oh my goodness.

CB: Kids are kids. We grow, but unfortunately some teachers treat you like adults. Kids process information differently than adults. What I was hearing was that "I am wrong/I do not belong." At the heart, education is about empowerment. I had to empower and encourage myself to keep going. Rejection helped my understanding and need of the choreographic voice.

NS: OK, wonderful. Do you prefer live musicians or tape?

CB: Live.

NS: What instruments?

CB: It depends on the story I'm trying to tell. For *ink*, since the story was rooted in the African diaspora, percussion is the primary instrument. For *Black Girl*, I wanted to show time travel—a visitation of the past— our childhood. For *Mr. TOL E. RAncE* [2012], since the piece was about stereotypes and minstrelsy, I wanted a piano riffing in and out of Scott Joplin–esque sounds.

Scott Patterson has been the lead collaborator and he's a brilliant composer and musician. Music is a storyteller and often the driving force. It informs everything—how people dance, interact, and evolve—so it's really important to me. Even though my process is challenging, there's nothing like being in the rehearsal space with live musicians creating and discovering alongside you.

NS: Yes.

CB: We're not in separate rooms but creating together. Live music is timeless, liberating, and uniquely its own voice. I listen differently when the music is live. There are so many ways to tell the story, and because it's organic, it's freeing but incredibly meticulous and controlled.

NS: When you work in a commercial area, how do you feel? Do you feel constricted, or do you feel free? Do you feel challenged by the different mechanisms like a camera or by stage lights? How does all this equipment affect you?

CB: The only commercial thing I've done is *Jesus Christ Superstar*, and I was scared out of my mind because I had never done television before.

NS: But it was beautiful. It was just beautiful.

CB: Thank you! I told myself, "You know, Camille, this is your first time doing TV and that's OK. The stuff you don't know, you'll learn. The only caveat is you have to learn it as fast as possible, and act like you knew it all along." (Laughs)

NS: OK.

CB: I had to make quick decisions and really trust my first instincts, because there was no time. David Leveaux, the director, created a real community. It wasn't about the glitz and glam of TV, but a real theatrically staged show. It wasn't until we got on set with the lights and cameras, that we realized *JCS* would be seen by millions. I was surrounded by veterans on the creative team who could have easily made me feel like the "new kid on the block," but I had constant support and encouragement. I've experienced situations where people made it very clear I was new. For *JCS*, I was given the agency to be OK not knowing it all because everyone—thankfully—believed in my work. It was one of the best experiences I've ever had.

NS: Didn't you do *Once on This Island*? How was that?

CB: I did! That was another first! First musical on Broadway and the show was done "in the round"— which I had never done before. It was exciting but extremely tough because I got sick during the process. My appendix ruptured on tour. This year alone, I've been in the hospital at least four times. I had two premieres scheduled a month after surgery: *ink* at the Kennedy Center and *Once on This Island* on Broadway.

NS: Oh my God.

CB: I almost died, so this year has been about recuperating. As a performer, I haven't felt in my body since 2016 because at the top of 2017, that's when everything started happening. While working on various projects and dealing with a health crisis, I feared my work would suffer and that it would be a reflection of my personal health struggles.

NS: I don't think it did either.

CB: Thank you for that! I'm thankful for my choreography team: Rickey Tripp, associate, and Catherine Foster, assistant. They protected my work.

NS: So building team is one of your strengths?

CB: We never do anything alone. Every director, choreographer, lighting designer, etc., have people who help them. My team supports me intellectually and emotionally too. My perspective is being challenged in the best of ways. Challenges help me be a better choreographer.

NS: One of the things that is fascinating is your determination to build an institution and to help others build an institution to keep the work going on and on. What set you on that path?

CB: It's how I was raised. If I'm eating, we're all eating. If I get a door open, it's my responsibility to make it wider.

NS: You definitely give back.

CB: Thank you! People ask me what is the hardest thing about being a choreographer. It's self-care and running a business. People see your success, but not many people are privy to the emotional shifts. Rejection still happens and hurts. Exhaustion is real. The importance of leadership and cultivating leaders is important. There are many times where I feel defeated and my company picks me back up. Regardless of whether I feel like a leader, I know I'm seen as one. That's a huge amount of responsibility to hold. I know, I went on a tangent

NS: No, no, it's OK because I had that experience today. I was asked [at a dance forum] to define my greatest fear and what I want on the other side of it, and my greatest fear is fear. I'm afraid of fear. I want freedom— that's what I want is freedom. But that was before they knew I was Ntozake Shange. They went around and they found out I was Notzake Shange. They were like, "You're afraid?" "Yes," that's what I said, that's what I meant.

CB: Because you ignite so much power in other people. It's hard to believe that someone who inspires us to be liberated still has fear.

NS: That's the same thing your dancers were telling me, that you inspire them. No matter how you feel about yourself, you inspire them. Despite all the other stuff that's going on.

CB: Right.

NS: It's the exact same thing, just a different situation.

CB: Yeah.

NS: This has been wonderful.

CB: This is a dream. Thank you!

This interview is revised and modified from the original.

DAVALOIS FEARON

NTOZAKE SHANGE: Who do you consider to be your mentor and why?

DAVALOIS FEARON: Well, the first person that comes to mind is Charmaine Warren. She's a wonderful mentor—I call her my dance mom.

NS: Where is she from?

DF: Charmaine is originally from Jamaica, like myself, and currently she lives in Montclair [, New Jersey]. I first met her through dancing with the Stephen Petronio Company. She's a writer and a performer, very well respected in the dance world, and she has a PhD, which is fabulous. I became more acquainted with her through Gino Grenek. He and Charmaine know each other very well. Charmaine would bring Gino to talk with the Ailey students about life as a professional dancer. He would say to me, "You've got to meet my friend

Charmaine, you've got to meet my friend Charmaine. She's amazing. You are going to love her." And he was right. When I met her, I did love her. She would always come to see the Petronio Company perform, so when I started choreographing I invited her to a showing. She actually booked me for E-moves, which she curated for many years. It is a Harlem Stage commission of new work that has a mentorship component. Nia Love was my fabulous mentor. After that program ended, I continued my relationship with Charmaine, and she's just been such a great mentor. I often call her and ask her a bunch of questions, like how do I handle this situation, and what would I do about that situation?

NS: What kind of dance does Charmaine do?

DF: So, Charmaine used to dance with David Roussève.

NS: I don't know who David Roussève is, but tell me about how he influenced her.

DF: I think through his approach to dance. He takes a postmodern approach to dance in terms of breaking away from the Western tradition of shape-oriented moves alone, like ballet, and instead allowing the body to move how the body wants to move. I had the pleasure of performing with [Charmaine] along with other African American dancers and a musician. The performance won us all Bessie Awards [the New York Dance and Performance Awards]! The performance was put together by Eva Yaa Asantewaa, an amazing writer and curator. My husband saw the show and said Charmaine and Nia were so fearless compared to everyone else. Everyone else was closer to my age, like in their thirties and forties, and maybe their late twenties. But my husband said that compared to Charmaine and Nia, we couldn't hold a candle to them. He said they were free and performed with complete abandon in terms of their ability to let go and let the body just do what it does, where he said he can see in the younger generation that we're just not there yet.

NS: What did he mean?

DF: From my perspective, I think there are choices that I questioned or I pulled back from letting go of self-consciousness. I was able to get to a free place during many parts of the performance. From my husband's perspective, Nia and Charmaine were there the whole time. That performance really opened me up to performing in a way I have never performed before.

NS: And the name of that performance was?

DF: *The skeleton architecture, or the future of our worlds.* It was put together to kind of make a statement, because there were the platforms curated by Will Rawls and Ishmael Houston-Jones, and they said, "We need a Black female, yeah that's the one thing that's missing from our curation." They called [Eva Yaa Asantewaa] and said, "Can you help us out? We're lacking in . . . Black female representation," and she said, "Oh you don't know where the Black female artists are? Well let me help you." She helped them put together this long, amazing list of dancers to kind of say, "Well there they are; we've always been here."

NS: Can you name some?

DF: Nia Love, Maria Bauman, Paloma McGregor, Sidra Bell, Charmaine Warren, Melanie Greene, Marguerite Hemmings are a couple of them. Kayla [Hamilton], there's Grace [Osborne], there's Marýa Wethers—those are the ones I can think of.

NS: So she had, like, a town then?

DF: Oh yeah.

NS: That sounds very powerful.

DF: That's what everyone said. Many said they've never experienced a performance like that. And I was so lucky to be a part of it, and I was changed after it. Because I had never felt the power of that many Black artists, and the majority of us identify as female and some are gender nonconforming. Having that power in the room was electric. It was so electric.

NS: Oh my goodness.

DF: And we made history that night because I don't think anything like that had ever been done with that many Black female and gender-nonconforming artists coming together from different walks of the dance world and improvising for two hours.

NS: Wow . . . oh my goodness. So when you were young, how did you start?

DF: Wow, well, like I said I was born in Jamaica, and Jamaican culture has dance and music embedded into the culture, so my family always tells stories about me coming out of the womb dancing. My mom said my dad gave me a bath one time before I could walk—some Jamaicans hold their kids upside down. They hold them by the ankles to help them grow, but I guess it didn't work because I'm only 5'4". I ended up crawling up backwards to look at him, and he was freaked out because I was his fifth child and the only one to do that. He called my mother and he was like, "Look," and I did it on cue. So my mom was like, "Oh my goodness, we have an unusual kid here." So whatever family member would come over, I would like to climb the walls all the way up to the top, and I forced my older sister to perform with me whenever family came over. I was always dancing and performing and lucky enough that the Alvin Ailey school actually did a program for eight weeks in the South Bronx—free dance classes. It was just enough to expose me to ballet, so when I went to audition for the Professional Performing Arts School, I was able to kind of keep up, and then the rest was history. I didn't even realize how much being taught by Black teachers and being surrounded by Black dancers would really set me up for success at that time. I now know it's sunk in, but I don't think back then I really

understood it. I didn't understand how special that
experience was. So when I went to Purchase College,
it was a culture shock because there were hardly any
Black people. I got into Petronio, and there were no
Black people in the company when I was hired.

NS: Who at Ailey stood out for you?

DF: Sharon Wong. She was my favorite teacher. She
taught jazz, and she gave me a hard time, surprisingly.
You would think your favorite teacher should be easy
on you, but she wasn't. I think it's because she knew my
potential, and I really have to give it up to her because
she took a lot of time crafting me as a young dancer.
When I started as a freshman at the Professional Performing Arts High School, I was just beginning my
training to be a professional dancer, compared to some
of my classmates who had been training since the age
of two. She was on top of me, and I graduated with
an advanced achievement in dance award. I had the
pleasure of taking class with Miss Katherine Dunham,
and I remember feeling like this is *the* Katherine
Dunham—

NS: *The* Katherine Dunham?

DF: And I don't think I really appreciated it. Definitely
that stood out to me. And Troy Powell, who is now the
director of Ailey II. He choreographed my last piece
in school. And then, of course, all the Ailey dancers. When you're in the junior division, you get to see
shows all the time from backstage. I remember helping

to bring out flowers to the dancers, and I think it was
Renee [Robinson]. She and Hope [Boykin] were in the
company—and Linda [Celeste Sims], who still is in the
company, and she's from the Bronx. Those three were
some of my favorites..

NS: So you have a company of your own.
What's that like?

DF: It's a lot of work! It's so much work, but I love it.

NS: What are the basic things you have to do to keep
a company together?

DF: OK, you definitely have to have support. I'm very
fortunate to have a Pentacle art fellowship, which gives
me an administrator ten hours a week and a mentor. And they help me with writing grants, they help
with fundraising, they help me with the marketing so
I can have an online presence—the website, the press
releases, social media. And then I work with a project manager who does the dancers' calendars and the
contracts, and she makes sure that they get paid. So
she kind of does a lot. So you have to have someone
managing the dancers, managing the finances, fund-
ing the company, and promoting the company, and the
other factor is the booking. I end up doing that a lot of
the time because it's about who you know, and I end up
reaching out to venues and invite people to rehearsals
and performances so that the word gets out there. So
yeah, booking, development, general operations, managing the dancers.

NS: When you say development, what do you mean?

DF: Development is like grant writing and also cultivating support from a community of organizations who believe in your mission. And it also involves individuals who contribute or make donations. One of the donors is a restaurateur, so he may contribute a dinner at the restaurant for a night as an item for the company to auction off at a fund-raiser, for example. Development is continually bringing in resources.

NS: It sounds like a lot to be in charge of at one time.

DF: And it's the juggling—once you pay attention to one area, other stuff starts falling apart in another area, but I love it.

NS: Are you willing to share your process?

DF: Yes. So the first piece that I made actually came through a conversation with a UN ambassador. He found me because he came to see a Petronio Company performance. He reached out to me and we started talking about him getting ready to go to Tajikistan to be the keynote speaker on water issues. I was like, I know a lot about that being from Jamaica—there's a lot of water scarcity. My sister had just recently paid to have water sent out to my family. He said, "Wow, aside from buying water, what are you doing about this water crisis?" I told him, "I don't have money; I can't solve this water issue," then instantly it snapped in my brain that I have dance. I can use dance as a platform for change. I can use that resource to spread awareness and get closer to the people that can actually put money there. And that was what set me on my path.

So my process is really driven by personal experience. It makes me ask a lot of questions, and from the questions I do a lot of research. I did a bunch of research on the privatization of water, where water comes from, when and how, and who has control over it, and we need to fight to make [access to] it a human right. So, I learned so much about that and I took that information into the studio and I remember I had the pages of print-outs with different images of water, different poems about water. I created a storyline in my head at first that touched on the different issues, from water scarcity to conflicts and wars over water to natural disasters like Katrina. I started looking at ways in which we as individuals can try to make a difference. Thinking about that storyline is how I've decide to say, OK, I'm going to have solos and duets that shift from water in abundance to none at all and end with a storm section here. I did, like, really aggressive, strong, striking moves to embody the ferocity of the storm. Then there was a solo that took place in a two-foot circle. It was really constricted, and we had to make small movements. And then the conflict, that was a duet—people fighting over water resources. Yeah, it's so rich.

NS: Sounds like it.

DF: And the current piece I'm working on is sadly inspired by my nephew who passed away from an asthma attack; he was twenty years old.

NS: Oh my.

DF: Yeah. I was so distraught. I just wanted to know
how could this happen, because I have asthma, and
I have to be honest, I never thought of it as a disease
that could kill. I started doing the research and I found
out how much medical racism, environmental racism,
and economic racism leads people to these areas where
they're exposed to a lot of these diseases or they're in
housing situations that are infested with roaches or
rats. Their droppings are poisonous, and it's one of the
contributors to asthma. And mold. So growing up in a
place where those things aren't attended to, you're living in an environment that every way you turn the air
you're breathing in is toxic. And you can't see it; it's so
embedded. We partnered with nonprofit organizations
like Bronx Health REACH, bringing the information
and the research that they have to the communities
that are the most affected, like the community my
nephew is from, in North Bronx. For this particular
piece I'm in the process of creating a work that's really
abstract. It's more abstract than my other work, which
has been very narrative driven. This piece still has that
narration because I love telling stories with dance. I use
the metaphor of the tree because I was also commissioned by the Bronx Museum to do an ode to [Gordon]
Matta-Clark, the visual artist. He went into abandoned
buildings in the Bronx to show how forgotten these
buildings and these people were in New York at that
time. So he also then created a piece that was in a tree,
and the dance interacted with the tree. We will try
to discover what makes space alive, and so that com-

bined with my nephew story—I looked at the Black body as a tree. I was thinking about the circle of life and death and how we grow out of the ground toward the sky, and then we fall and go back into the earth and then come back again. One of the dancers starts on the ground and grows up into a tree. It's always a personal impact that sets me on my journey, followed by research and then going into the studio and using dance to tell the story.

NS: That's very interesting, because that's the way they work in Cuba.

DF: Oh, really?

NS: Yes, they call us cultural workers, and they send you to the factory, to the cane fields, or to schools or to buildings. Then . . . you interview people and you do the research. You put all that together and you make your art.

DF: Oh, wow.

NS: It sounds very much like what you do. Think about it. So of the pieces that you mentioned, do you consider one of them your signature piece?

DF: I think the *Time to Talk* piece because that's a solo, and it's definitely a piece that says, "Here I am." It's a little autobiographical. I go from my Jamaican roots through some reggae, and my husband, who is white, he'll say, "Oh no, you can't do that, but I have something for you." Then he'll give me a bag, and it'll be a bag of ballet shoes. So we'll do ballet. Then he gives me a bag of modern; then I do modern dance. At a point I start to question that divide between one way and another way. That's the piece that really shows my aesthetic and how I move. Modern, ballet, and a little bit of Jamaica.

NS: OK, wow. That sounds great. Did you find that you had to dance, and did you find that you had to be a choreographer?

DF: Well you know I think that's a divide between the Jamaican diva and the diva who started really focusing on being a professional dancer. My creative diva was putting on shows for my family, and I stopped doing that once I started training. And it wasn't until I met my husband—he saw that I had all this creative energy. I said, "Oh I'm going to be a psychologist." I was going to dance for ten years and then I was going to get a real job because my Jamaican immigrant parents were worried about me making a living. He was like, "You're going to do what? No, give me a break." He had a concert coming up, and he said, "You know I have this music that I really think would look beautiful with dance, if only I knew a choreographer . . ."

I totally fell for it, and I said, "OK, fine." I was petrified to put my own work on stage. I ran into the UN ambassador and that was the first time that I unlocked that door that was closed when I was a kid. And at that moment I was like, "I am a choreographer; I've always been a choreographer. I just lost touch with that young diva that was doing that. I was born doing it and it didn't get nurtured." For dance the men tend to end up choreographing more than the women, and we're taught to be the perfect empty vessels. The choreographer comes in and tells us what to do and we jump right in line, and I was good at that. But once I unlocked that door, it was just like, of course. And I can bring in my passion for wanting to help people and the psychology in the dance. So, you know, it wasn't apparent to me, but it was apparent to everyone around me, and when they found out I was choreographing they said of course.

NS: Do you like to work with live musicians or recording?

DF: Live musicians.

NS: Like what?

DF: You know I'm spoiled, right? My husband plays piano, saxophone, clarinet, flute. The first time we worked together, he got this chamber ensemble: a bassoon, violin, clarinet. I like recorded music, but with live music you have to be on your toes, you know, because sometimes they'll stretch out that note. That is so fun in terms of you have to really be in the moment. There's a different kind of presence and an awareness that live music brings.

NS: Do you do any commercial work?

DF: I did in the past. I'm not that great at it. I danced in *An Ode To* with Solange at the Guggenheim. I took a year off to do some Broadway and some hip-hop. Yeah, those people [at the Guggenheim] are amazing; they can improvise with hip-hop. I can try and reconnect with that monster, but now I'm happy with concert.

NS: That's important.

AFTERWORD

I HAD THE DISTINCT honor and privilege of working with Ntozake Shange from the summer of 2014 until her unexpected transition on October 27, 2018. By profession, I am a theater professor, actor, and director who teaches the work of luminaries like Ntozake, but I had never dreamed of living life alongside such a public figure until my time with her.

I was familiar with her legacy and introduced to her work in an undergraduate African American literature class. Fast-forward almost twenty years later, I was at the National Black Theatre Festival waiting in line for her to autograph my newly purchased copy of her novel *Betsey Brown*. We spoke briefly but only in regard to how I wanted her to autograph the book. So when I formally met her, as I assisted behind the scenes for a staged reading of *for colored girls* at the fortieth-anniversary celebration in New York, I was, to say the least, ecstatic. Through a series of fortunate events, and a bit of fate, I spent three and half years accompanying Ntozake during her travels and appearances. Despite her health challenges, she was always eager to craft a poem, pen a story, write a book, or create a movement. I witnessed firsthand her passion for the arts and her genuine concern for social issues as they pertained to disenfranchised groups.

Ntozake's priority was always her writing. She told me that when she was younger, she would sit and type for days on end and only take breaks to drink coffee or have an occasional bite to eat. She felt writing was a *physical* process and said she would often sweat while she wrote because her work was so intense and mentally taxing. After her strokes, she had limited use of her hands. However, her passion for creating was so powerful that she would handwrite her choreopoems and choreoessays, often to the point of debilitating pain. Her attention was never far from a news story or something she read that was inspiring or spoke to her. One day she called to say she had typed one of her first poems since the last stroke. It was a poem about the shootings at the Pulse nightclub in Orlando. Using her iPad, she created this poem one letter at a time. I was driving, but when she told me about the accomplishment, I pulled over so we could cry and celebrate together. She was so elated to be able to type again.

After the completion of *Wild Beauty: New and Selected Poems*, in 2017, we began to work on *Dance We Do*. There were quite a few moving parts to the book because she originally started the book during her time in Florida in the early 1990s, but it was placed on hold after she became ill. The previous pieces she'd written needed to be organized and edited, but her objective remained clear. She envisioned personal profiles of each dancer, interviews of the dancers along with a glossary of terms to guide laypeople. This was an extensive project, but she was up for the challenge. Our typical workday consisted of her telling me whom she wanted to profile, my asking her how she met that person, and her telling me these wonderful stories. Sometimes she would sit on her bed and begin to talk, reminiscing about a dance concert, a dance rehearsal, or a dance performance. I found it amazing how she could recall with such detail an experience in such colorful terms. She told stories of dancing to the music of legendary bandleaders and going to auditions in New York while dodging panhandlers. These history lessons were so intriguing, I would forget I was supposed to type. Later, during my transcribing, I realized I had missed sections of the story, and she and I would have to go back and fill in the blanks. Finally, my daughter suggested recording Ms. Shange and typing it later. These accounts of our time together are now priceless to me.

While this book is one of the final works she penned, it is not entirely complete. We did not have the opportunity to interview and observe the work of many of her esteemed dance colleagues. Travel plans were in place, and appointments for us to observe rehearsals had been arranged. However, she made her transition before we were able to meet with and ultimately include in the book such greats as George Faison, Jawole Willa Jo Zollar, Bill T. Jones, Amaniyea Payne, Stanze Peterson, Chuck Davis, Titos Sompa, Okwui Okpokwasili, Da' Von Doane, Loremil Machado, Donald McKayle, and Anna Glass. Others such as Camille Brown, Davalois Fearon, and Dyane Harvey were interviewed, but her personal portraits of them remain incomplete.

Ntozake's career spanned over fifty years and consisted of writing, acting, dancing, speaking, performing, directing, and teaching. She was a trailblazer in the world of feminism and women's studies, and openly took on topics others dared not broach. Her collaborators included giants in the business of theater, dance, and art, yet she found time to travel, spend time with family, and stay abreast of current events.

Many mornings I would arrive at her house and she was earlobe deep in a broadcast of *Morning Joe* or *MSNBC Live*, and would spend an hour discussing the goings-on in the world of politics and culture. When we traveled, she would fall asleep to Chris Cuomo, Anderson Cooper, or Don Lemon playing in the background. Moreover, I would be remiss not to mention the constant Pepsi consumption that seemed to fuel her writer's spirit.

Writing and publishing this book was of the utmost importance to Ntozake, mainly because she felt it was so needed. Currently, there is a lack of literature that chronicles the contributions of Black professional dancers, and Ntozake wished to fill this void. She once told me, "Through dance, I found a way to further express myself, and I used it. I combined two of my favorite art forms . . . dance and poetry." This was the creation of the choreopoem. She defined choreopoem as "a series of poems, with occasional music and dance," which when all put together becomes a statement, a voice. This book was her baby, and she was excited to share something different for her in terms of artistic content yet familiar to her in terms of her artistic practice with her readers.

Ntozake, thank you. Thank you for the friendship, the poetry, the dance, and the artistry. Thank you for the mentorship, the activism, the creativity, the audacity, and the honesty. And thank you for the gifts of self-love and hope you gave one little Southern Black girl who found god in herself too.

Ase Queen, Ase.

—RENEÉ L. CHARLOW, DECEMBER 2019

BIOGRAPHIES OF DANCERS AND CHOREOGRAPHERS

MICKEY DAVIDSON

FRED BENJAMIN was chair of the Jazz Department and a faculty advisor at the Alvin Ailey American Dance Theater. An internationally recognized choreographer of jazz dance, his artistic affiliations included IAC Studio in Tokyo, New York's Clark Center for the Performing Arts, and the Vlaamse Dansacademie, Brugge, Belgium. He also taught at the State University of New York, Purchase; the American Dance Festival; and Jacob's Pillow, Lee, Massachusetts. He founded the Fred Benjamin Dance Company in 1968 while performing on Broadway. The company performed extensively in the US and the Caribbean until 1990. His choreography for other companies includes *Ice Fire* for Alvin Ailey Repertory Ensemble and *After the Rain* for Impulse Dance Company, Boston. He taught until his death in 2013.

CAMILLE A. BROWN is a prolific Black female director and choreographer reclaiming the cultural narrative of the African American identity. She is the recipient of numerous awards and honors, including Tony and Drama Desk nominations for her work on Tarell Alvin McCraney's *Choir Boy* on Broadway, a Guggenheim fellowship, and a Doris Duke Artist Award. Her choreography credits include the Alvin Ailey American Dance Theater, the Tony Award–winning *Once on This Island*, Ntozake Shange's *for colored girls who have considered suicide/when the rainbow is enuf*, and the Netflix production of August Wilson's *Ma Rainey's Black Bottom*. She is the founder and artistic director of her Bessie Award–winning company Camille A. Brown & Dancers.

MICKEY DAVIDSON is a distinguished dancer and choreographer. Her dance career has been the study and performance of African American historical dance styles and includes working with Sounds in Motion dance company, Sun Ra, Jeanne Lee, and poet/playwright Ntozake Shange for over thirty years. The Shange-Davidson artistic relationship comprised several collaborations, including the twentieth-anniversary production of *for colored girls who have considered suicide/when the rainbow is enuf*, produced by the New Federal Theatre and directed by Ntozake Shange. Davidson is the primary choreographer for her company, Mickey D & Friends. She has been teaching American History through Jazz Dance for over forty years in educational and community institutions.

DAVALOIS FEARON is a critically acclaimed choreographer, dancer, and educator, born in Jamaica and raised in the Bronx. She is a recipient of the prestigious MAP Fund Grant, received a Bessie Award for her performance in *the skeleton architecture, or the future of our worlds*, and was named among "7 Up-and-Coming Black Dance Artists Who Should Be on Your Radar" by *Dance Magazine*. Her choreography, which was said by *Dance Magazine* to reflect a "tenacious virtuosity," has been presented nationally and internationally, including at renowned venues such as the Joyce Theater and the Metropolitan Museum of Art.

DYANE HARVEY is a performing artist, educator, and choreographer. She is a founding member of the Forces of Nature Dance Theatre, a Harlem-based company whose mission is audience empowerment with a focus on the preservation of this planet. Harvey currently serves as the assistant to the director, Abdel R. Salaam, who is also her collaborator and husband. She has performed with the concert dance companies of Eleo Pomare, George Faison, Otis Sallid, and others, which prepared her for a career on and off Broadway. Her experiences ultimately paved the way for an inspirational collaborative relationship with Ntozake Shange. She was an original cast member for *Spell #7* and *Boogie Woogie Landscapes*, as well as the choreographer for *Hydraulics Phat Like Mean* and *Lavender Lizards and Lilac Landmines: Layla's Dream*.

DIANNE MCINTYRE is a dancer and choreographer whose Harlem-based company Sounds in Motion was founded in 1972 and who creates works for concert dance, Broadway, and regional theater. Her screen credits include *Beloved* and *Miss Evers' Boys* (Emmy Award nomination). Among her honors are a Doris Duke Artist Award, a Guggenheim fellowship, two honorary degrees, and numerous grants. She collaborated and choreographed with Ntozake Shange on many projects, including *Spell #7*, *Boogie Woogie Landscapes*, *Why I Had to Dance*, *Lost in Language and Sound*, and more.

ED MOCK, a dancer, choreographer, and instructor, melded classical dance, experimental performance art, and acting. He was a major part of San Francisco's awakening as an arts hub before his death in 1986. Under the tutelage of the celebrated

Jimmy Payne in Chicago, Mock refined his craft and performed internationally for decades. His style pushed boundaries with his improvisational techniques, nude and gender-fluid performances, and mesmerizing genre-defying dance. During a time when New York dance often emphasized hard lines and performer compliance, Mock had a characteristically different San Francisco approach. His classes, performances, and dance company emphasized the humanity and unique personality of each individual, which made space for everyone's artistic ability within the collective.

PAULA MOSS has been shaping the lives of children and adults in Rome through hatha yoga for the past thirty years. A native of San Francisco, Moss began her dance career at the age of thirteen with Ed Mock before studying modern, classical, and jazz dance at the University of California, Irvine. Throughout the 1970s Moss danced with many companies, including Agnes De Mille, American Heritage Theater, Dream on Monkey Mountain, and the Alvin Ailey junior company. In 1973 Moss met Raymond Sawyer and joined his dance company. At this time, she also met her lifelong friend and future collaborator Ntozake Shange. What began as dancing alongside Shange during her poetry readings evolved into choreographing the original 1976 production of *for colored girls who have considered suicide/when the rainbow is enuf* and performing as the Lady in Green for its early performances at the Public Theater. In 1976 Moss encountered her guru, Swami Muktananda, and studied with him until his passing in 1982. In 1990 Moss moved to Rome, where she currently lives with her family and teaches hatha yoga.

HALIFU OSUMARE has been involved with dance and Black popular culture internationally for over forty years as a dancer, choreographer, teacher, administrator, and scholar. She is professor emerita of African American and African studies at the University of California, Davis, and has written two books on global hip-hop and a memoir, *Dancing in Blackness.* As an artist and dance activist, Dr. Osumare was a soloist with the Rod Rodgers Dance Company; was the founder and former co-director of Oakland's first multi-ethnic dance institution, Everybody's Creative Arts Center (now the Malonga Casquelourd Center for the Arts); and is a certified instructor for Dunham Technique Certification, which continues the legacy of dancer-anthropologist Katherine Dunham.

ELEO POMARE was an internationally renowned master choreographer whose works reflect a broad humanistic perspective and a commitment to social change. His classic works include *Las Desenamoradas, Blues for the Jungle, Missa Luba, Hex*, and *Roots.* Along with leading the Eleo Pomare Dance Company in New York City, he choreographed works for the Alvin Ailey American Dance Theater and numerous other companies in the US and throughout Europe, Australia, Asia, and South America. His numerous awards include a Guggenheim Fellowship, being named a Kennedy Center Master of African American Choreography, the James Baldwin Award, the International Association of Blacks in Dance Outstanding Achievements Award, and the January 7, 1987, declaration of Eleo Pomare Day in honor of his contributions to the cultural life of New York City. Born in Colombia and raised in New York City, he graduated from the High School of Performing Arts. A John Hay Whitney Fellowship took him to Europe, where he studied, danced, and choreographed for two years. Returning to New York in 1964, he established the Eleo Pomare Dance Company, which toured the US, Canada, the Caribbean, Europe, and Africa and performed in major venues like New York City Center, the Joyce Theater, and the Kennedy Center for the Performing Arts. Some of his featured dancers included Dudley Williams, Loretta Abbott, Al Perryman, Dyane Harvey, Charles Grant, Chuck Davis, Martial Roumain, Carl Paris, Leni Wylliams, and Diana Ramos.

OTIS SALLID is a director, choreographer, and producer whose accomplishments in theater, television, and film are known throughout the entertainment industry. After graduating from Juilliard, he worked as an actor and dancer for numerous Broadway shows and dance companies before launching his production company, Creative Otis Inc. As a choreographer and director he has worked on countless productions, shows, and films, including Spike Lee's *School Daze, Do the Right Thing*, and *Malcolm X*, as well as *Living Single, Sister Act II*, the Sixty-Ninth Academy Awards, Debbie Allen's *Fame*, the Super Bowl XV Halftime Show, and Mariah Carey's *All I Want for Christmas Is You* at the Beacon Theatre in New York. Sallid is the recipient of numerous awards, including several Tony Award nominations, an MTV Music Video Award, and a Grammy Award.

RAYMOND SAWYER (born Raymond S. Robinson) was raised in New York City. He had extensive dance training in ballet, modern, and Afro-Haitian dance. In the early 1960s he studied at the New Dance Group in Donald McKayle's popular classes alongside Eleo Pomare, Diana Ramos, and Dudley Williams. He performed in Pomare's very first concerts. Also, in New York City he had his own dance company and produced an early concert (1967) at the Fashion Institute of Technology. (Prior to his New York dance career, he taught youth at an interracial summer camp in Monteagle, Tennessee). After teaching in Boston, where he formed the performing arts company the Third Eye, he moved to San Francisco. There he taught his own unique style of dance at various universities in the Northern California area and between 1969 and 1970 he founded the Black Dance Institute in San Francisco. He also directed his own company there and performed in dance productions of Halifu Osumare. After a near-death experience, Raymond began practicing Buddhism and at the invitation of Carole Johnson moved to Australia in the mid-1980s. He taught and choreographed for NAISDA (National Aboriginal and Islander Skills and Development Association) and NAISDA Dance College. When it was time to form an independent professional Indigenous dance company with graduates of NAISDA, Raymond became the artistic coordinator, and the company took the name Bangarra Dance Theatre Australia. He coordinated it from 1989 to 1991. Later he was accepted into the master's program at Nepean University in Sydney, where he did extensive research on the history of Aboriginal dancing. His work *Dreaming Tracks* was pioneering in the field and was presented just before his death in 2004. The name "Wanaga" was given to him by the Aboriginal people.

Some information contained in these biographies is from the following sources: "Faculty Bio: Fred Benjamin (1944–2013): Steps on Broadway: Jazz," Steps on Broadway, 2020, https://www.stepsnyc.com/faculty/bio/Fred-Benjamin; Anna Kisselgoff, "Fred Benjamin, Exacting and Inventive Teacher of Jazz Dance, Dies at 69," *New York Times*, Dec. 19, 2013, https://www.nytimes.com/2013/12/20/arts/dance/fred-benjamin-teacher-of-jazz-dance-dies-at-69.html; *Unstoppable Feat: The Dances of Ed Mock*, framline.org, 2017, https://www.frameline.org/festival/festival-archive/festival2018/film-guide/unstoppable-feat-the-dances-of-ed-mock; Great Performances: Free to Dance, Biographies: Eleo Pomare, WNET, https.thirteen.org/freetodance/biographies/pomare.html, accessed Jan. 5, 2020.

GLOSSARY

MICKEY DAVIDSON, DIANNE MCINTYRE,
AND HALIFU OSUMARE

ACE IN THE HOLE. A dance step that goes up in the air.

APOGEE. The highest point in the development of something, a climax or culmination.

ASSEMBLÉ. After pushing off both feet to jump in the air with one leg higher to the side, assemblé is the motion of landing after that jump with the feet together on the floor usually in the fifth position (feet flat and turned out with the heel of one foot touching the big toe of the other foot).

ATTITUDE JETÉS. *Jeté* means *throw*. In dance, this is a throwing of the leg: a leaping jump from one foot to the other. Throw one leg up and push off the opposite foot to rise up in the air (leap) and land on the thrown leg. With this leap, the back leg (the pushing-off leg) is bent and lifted to the back, with the knee ideally bent at a 90-degree angle and the knee up higher than the foot in the back.

BATTEMENT. This is a lift, kick, or swing of the leg up in the air with the knee straight.

BLACK VERNACULAR DANCE. These are dances that originate among Black folks and are native to the group. The term is often used interchangeably with *Black social dance*, but *vernacular* is a more all-encompassing term than *social partnering dance*; *vernacular* can refer to dances such as the buck dance, a precursor to tap dance and which was an exhibition of skilled rhythmic movement by virtuosos, as opposed to social dances that everyone performed.

BOOGALOO (ALSO *BUGALOO*). A fast dance of African American origin, performed by couples and characterized by dancing apart and moving the body in short, quick movements to the beat of the music.

BOOGIE-WOOGIE. A musical genre associated with a Black piano style that emerged in the 1920s. It was eventually extended from piano to piano duos, and guitars, big band, country and western music, and even underpinned gospel music. There was also a kind of boogie-woogie dance that went with the music.

CAKEWALK. An African American dance that started on the slave plantation with a long historical trajectory, from coded high kicking movements satirizing the slave master to becoming the first American dance craze at the turn of the twentieth century. In its slave origins, Africans used to mimic how they saw European Americans' pompous body language and would stick out their chest and strut around in imitation of them as an inside joke. The dance eventually became the finale of the Black-face minstrel shows and a dance the Black middle class and the white upper class did at the beginning of the 1900s, having forgotten its original intent. The term *cakewalk* alludes to the fact that on the slave plantation, the dancers who kicked the highest would win a homemade cake, which was a delicacy given the slop slaves were usually fed.

CHARLESTON. A Black social dance that emerged in the 1920s. Some say it has Congolese origins and first started in Charleston, South Carolina, hence the name. The dance, which uses the crossing of the legs back and forth, was made famous at New York's Savoy Ballroom during the Jazz Age. As whites came uptown to patronize the live music and dancing at the Savoy, it quickly became the second American dance craze after the Cakewalk. Everybody was doing the Charleston in the 1920s moving into the 1930s.

CLOGGING. English folk dances with rhythmic use of the feet, while wearing English clog shoes. Also, a social dance in US Appalachia with ties to the early development of African American tap dancing.

CREOLE QUADRILLES. French square dances adapted in Caribbean countries including Dominica, Guadeloupe, and Saint Lucia. The adaptation represented a creolization of French social partner dances that Africanized the French style by using hip/pelvis movements, blending with upright formations of the quadrilles. The variations of the Creole quadrille showed the blending of European and African cultures in the Caribbean through dance.

DIAGONAL LINES. Going upstage left to downstage right, as opposed to moving laterally (left to right) or vertically (upstage straight down) in a dance class or onstage.

DUNHAM TECHNIQUE. The dance technique of the great dancer-anthropologist Katherine Dunham (1909–2006), one of the first African Americans to gain worldwide recognition in dance, formed the Katherine Dunham Dance Company in 1938. Her technique is the first fusion style that included classical ballet, modern dance, and Afro-Caribbean folk dance. One of the founders of dance anthropology, she did her master's degree dance research in the Caribbean in the mid-1930s and brought those styles back to the US, incorporating them into her creative dance approach in the development of her technique, which has been codified and is now in its fourth generation, with new generations of dancers able to be certified as instructors. The hallmark of the technique is two-fold: (1) the use of rhythmic torso isolations from head to hips, and (2) a wholistic approach that emphasizes mind, body, and spirit and integrates mind, body and spirit.

FIREBIRD. A dynamic solo figure in a famous ballet, *The Firebird*, choreographed in 1910 by Michael Fokine with music by Igor Stravinsky. It has been restaged by many choreographers over the years.

FIRST- AND SECOND-POSITION PLIÉS. *Plié* means bending of the knees. A first-position plié is one with the heels touching and the toes turned out, and you bend the knees from that position of the feet. A second-position plié is when the feet are in a wide stance one to two feet apart, and the bend of the knees is done from the position.

GRAND BATTEMENT. Lifting, swinging, or kicking the leg up very high with the knee straight.

GRAND CHASSÉ. *Grand* means *big*, and *chassé* means chase, so a *chassé* is when one foot chases the other foot out of its position, done in a series. repeated in the same direction. It could also be called a sliding step or a gallop. Grand chassés are a series of huge galloping movements in which one foot is chasing the other and the dancer is also elevating high off the floor. This series of movements involves traveling through space to the side, the front, or the back.

GRAND JETÉ LEAPS. Very high leaps with legs stretched out very long or bent in the air, as if leaping over a big puddle.

HORTON TECHNIQUE. A dance technique initiated by Lester Horton (1906–1953) in Los Angeles in 1946. His technique is based on Native American dances and anatomical studies. He established the Lester Horton Dance Theater and, besides Katherine Dunham, was one of the first to insist upon racial integration in his company. In his 1995 autobiography, Alvin Ailey, who took over the directorship of the company after Horton died, wrote, "What it came down to was that, for Lester, his art was much more important than the color of a dancer's skin." Ailey continued the Horton technique, which became the primary modern technique for his Alvin Ailey American Dance Theater.

JETÉ. A leap.

JITTERBUG. This was simply another name for the Lindy Hop, which became the third American dance craze, made famous in the 1930s, again at the Savoy Ballroom. The Lindy Hop, supposedly originated by Savoy dancer George "Shorty"

Snowden, was very up tempo, done to big band swing music, with fast-moving feet within partner dancing. One of the most influential Black contributions to American and world culture, expressing the liberation from the ground implied by Charles Lindbergh's solo transatlantic flight in 1927. People said that Lindy dancers moved so fast they looked like they had the jitters, hence the other name given to the dance, the Jitterbug.

MOCK TECHNIQUE. Ed Mock (c. 1938–1986) was a San Francisco Bay Area dancer who came to the city from Chicago. His work was often daring and experimental, genre and gender bending, and was at the forefront of the alternative West Coast dance scene in the 1970s, after he first came to San Francisco in 1966. His technique, which he taught at Gloria Unti's Performing Arts Workshop, was based on Afro-Cuban jazz, and he often used live drumming. There's a documentary about him called *Unstoppable Feat: The Dances of Ed Mock*, by Brontez Purnell.

PIROUETTES. This is a turn on one foot, a full 360-degree revolution.

PIROUETTES ON BOTH SIDES. Full turns on one foot and then a turn on the other foot or both sides.

PORT DE BRAS. The carriage of the arms in classical ballet. A *jazz port de bras* is arms up to side; then arms to chest, palms facing chest with elbows out; press arms straight up past the ears; open back to sides.

SAWYER TECHNIQUE. Raymond Sawyer was a dancer in the San Francisco Bay Area, from the late 1970s to the late 1980s, who had originally come from New York. His technique was a combination of modern, jazz, Dunham, and what he called Afro-American dance. He had a strong lyrical style and attracted many Black dancers during that period.

RING SHOUT. A song and movement ritual tradition with roots in Africa and brought into a Christian context during times of slavery. The shouters move counterclockwise in a ring as they sing, shuffle feet, and clap in interlocking rhythms. One person keeps the tempo, beating a stick onto wood planks as the energy of the shouters builds, sometimes to a religious fervor.

ROND DE JAMBE. *Jambe* is leg. While standing on one leg, the dancer makes the motion of a circle with the other leg, either tracing a circle on the floor with the toes or using a lifted leg to make the motion of a circle in the air.

SAND DANCING. A rhythmic dance done in sand and a confined space.

SECOND-POSITION RELEVÉ. This is when the feet are in a wide stance one to two feet apart and the dancer rises up to stand on the balls of the feet. This is a relevé on the Dunham and Horton ballet bar.

STAIR DANCE. A tap routine in which the person dances up and down stairs.

TERPSICHORES. Goddesses of dance, such as Elvia Marta, Cecilia Marta, Brenda Miller, Rosalie Alphonso, and Paula Moss. Brilliant dancers who own dance and live it.

A NOTE FROM THE NTOZAKE SHANGE REVOCABLE TRUST

All of Ntozake Shange's autobiographical, written, and spoken references to her "inspiration" cite the physical experience presented by her appearances onstage, dance classes, lectures, and interviews. These were the primary motivations for her writing. Accordingly, the Family and the Trustees of the Estate wish to express their deep gratitude to the following collaborators, sponsors, presenters, and close friends whose encouragement, promotion, and recognition of Ntozake's work powered her commitment to keep writing during the completion of *Dance We Do: A Poet Explores Black Dance*.

Gratefully,
Paul T. Williams Jr., Managing Trustee
Donald S. Sutton, Literary Trustee
The Ntozake Shange Revocable Trust

Harriet Shange-Watkins

Savannah Shange

Ifa Bayeza

Bisa Williams

Paul T. Williams Jr.

Ammie Felder-Williams

Voza Rivers

Mecca Jamilah Sullivan

Mariposa Fernandez

Lynn Nottage

Kamilah Forbes

Irene Gandy

Alexis Pauline Gumbs

Anna Glass

Sylvia White

Staceyann Chin

Karen Allen Baxter

Dr. Monica Ndounou

Henry Halle

Gaven Trinidad

Flemmie Kitrell and Robert Williams

Mandy Hackett

Camille Brown

Reneé L. Charlow

Leah Gardiner

Gail Papp

Logan Vaughn

Don Sutton

Jill Newman

Erich McMillan McCall

Marcia Pendelton

Sade Lythcott

Michael Dinwiddie

Ron Simons

Kim Hall

Shannon O'Neill

Helene Atwan

Zita Allen

Vincent Thomas

Cherine Anderson

Adger Cowans

Dr. Cassandra L. Jones

Jody Solomon

Jean Caiani

Rashid Johnson

Arturo Lindsay

Dawn Davis

Souleo

Rob McQuilkin

Abbie Van Nostrand

Kahil El'Zabar

Michael Denneny

Frank Stewart

KB Saine

Marco Hall

Olivier Sultan

Charly Palmer

Hyacinth Reynolds

Halima Taha

Abdel Salaam

Julieanna Richardson

Iana Dikidjieva

Paula Moss

Oz Scott

Oskar Eustis

Dyane Harvey

Dianne McIntyre

Regina Taylor

Woodie King Jr.

Tarana Burke

Thulani Davis

Oliver Lake

William "Spaceman" Patterson

Michele Shay

Trazana Beverley

Eugene Jensen

Martin Farawell

Alejandro Alvarez Nieves

Daniel David

Retha Powers

Ursula Day

Karen Brown

Jeremy Johnson

Dr. Johnetta Coles

Emily Underwood

Jill Soloway

Jessica Hagedorn

George Faison

Ishmael Reed

Oskar Eustis

PHOTO CREDITS

12. Photographer unknown. Courtesy of the Ntozake Shange Revocable Trust & Barnard College Archives and Special Collections.
13, 14, and 15. Photograph by Joan Marcus. Courtesy of the Ntozake Shange Revocable Trust & Barnard College Archives and Special Collections.

NOTES

FOREWORD

1. Ntozake Shange Collection, Barnard College Archives, box 2, folder 6.
2. Ntozake Shange Collection, Barnard College Archives, box 5, folder 2.
3. Ntozake Shange, *Lost in Language and Sound: Or How I Found My Way to the Arts* (New York: St. Martin's Press, 2011), 52.
4. Ntozake Shange and Dianne McIntyre, "In Conversation," Worlds of Shange, Barnard Center for Research on Women, New York, NY, February 14, 2013.
5. Shange and McIntyre, "In Conversation."
6. Shange and McIntyre, "In Conversation."
7. Ntozake Shange Collection, Barnard College Archives, box 19, folder 1.
8. Jamara Wakefield, "Ntozake Shange on Writing Her Own Words Her Own Way," *Shondaland*, December 14, 2017, https://www.shondaland .com/live/a13999488/ntozake-shange-interview.
9. Echoed reference to Alice Walker, "In Search of Our Mothers' Gardens," in Walker, *In Search of Our Mothers' Gardens: Womanist Prose* (San Diego, CA: Harcourt Brace Jovanovich, 1983).
10. Shange, *Lost in Language and Sound*, 89.
11. Shange, *Lost in Language and Sound*, 69.
12. Shange, *Lost in Language and Sound*, 135.
13. Ntozake Shange, *Liliane* (New York: Picador USA, 1994), 66.

14. Wakefield, "Ntozake Shange on Writing Her Own Words Her Own Way."

15. Ntozake Shange Collection, Barnard College Archives, box 5, folder 2.

16. Wakefield, "Ntozake Shange on Writing Her Own Words Her Own Way."

17. Ntozake Shange, *Wild Beauty: New and Selected Poems* (New York: Atria, 2017), 211.

18. Shange and McIntyre, "In Conversation."

19. Audre Lorde, "Poetry Is Not a Luxury," in Lorde, *Sister Outsider: Essays and Speeches* (Berkeley, CA: Crossing Press, 1984), 37.

20. "Skeleton Architecture," https://movementresearch.org/people/skeleton-architecture, accessed December 17, 2019.

21. Shange, *Lost in Language and Sound*, 51–58.

22. Ntozake Shange Collection, Barnard College Archives, box 19, folder 1.

23. Shange, *Lost in Language and Sound*, 41.

24. Ntozake Shange, "My Song for Hector Lavoe," in *Aloud: Voices from the Nuyorican Poets Café*, ed. Miguel Algarín and Bob Holman (New York: Holt and Co., 1994), 366.

ABOUT THE AUTHORS

NTOZAKE SHANGE (1948–2018) is an icon of American the-ater and Black women's performance and literature. *Ntozake* means "she who comes with her own things," in Xhosa, and *Shange* means "she who walks like a lion," in Zulu. Before tak-ing on this name in 1971, she was known as Paulette Williams. She grew up in Trenton, New Jersey, and St. Louis, Missouri. Her father was a surgeon, and her mother was an educator and psychiatric social worker.

In 1966, Shange enrolled at Barnard College, where she was active in the movement for Black studies and graduated cum laude in American studies in 1970. She earned a mas-ter's degree in American studies in 1973 from the University of Southern California.

While living in California, Shange danced with Halifu Osumare's company and performed in the San Francisco area. She worked with Paula Moss, who would later choreograph the original productions of the play *for colored girls who have con-sidered suicide/ when the rainbow is enuf.* Moss and Shange left California for New York and performed together in a Soho jazz loft and in bars on the Lower East Side. Producer Woodie King Jr. saw one of these and produced the debut of *for colored girls . . .* Off-Broadway at the New Federal Theatre, directed by Oz Scott. The play then moved to the New York Shakespeare Festival/Public Theatre, and then to Broadway at the Booth Theatre for 742 performances. It won the Obie Award and was nominated for a Tony and a Grammy.

In addition to fourteen plays, Shange is the author of four poetry collections, seven novels, and six children's books. She was honored as a Living Legend by the National Black Theatre Festival and also with the Langston Hughes Medal, the Hurston/Wright Award, two Obies, a Pushcart Prize, and countless other awards.

The revival of *for colored girls . . .* at the Public Theater in October 2019 ran for nine, sold-out weeks and swept the year's theatre awards. Ntozake Shange's legacy continues to impact multitudes. As Ifa Bayeza has put it: "I don't think there's a day on the planet when there's not a young woman who discovers herself through the words of my sister."

RENEÉ L. CHARLOW was personal assistant to Ntozake Shange from 2014 to 2018. She is an actor, director, writer, and theatre professor. She served as associate producer and assistant director for the production of Shange's *Lost in Language and Sound* at Karamu House, Cleveland, Ohio, and directed *for colored girls who have considered suicide/when the rainbow is enuf* at Virginia Commonwealth University and Bowie State University. Keep in touch with Reneé at mycreativespirit.net.

ALEXIS PAULINE GUMBS is the literary advisor to the Ntozake Shange Revocable Trust. She is the author of *M Archive: After the End of the World, Spill: Scenes of Black Feminist Fugitivity*, and *Dub: Finding Ceremony*. She is the co-editor of *Revolutionary Mothering: Love on the Front Lines* and the author of the forthcoming books *Undrowned* and *The Eternal Life of Audre Lorde.* Gumbs is the founder of Brilliance Remastered, an organization that supports underrepresented scholars, artists, and organizers. Alexis has received numerous awards and recognitions such as *The Advocate* magazine's 40 Under 40 and *Colorlines*'s 10 LGBTQ Leaders Transforming the South. Connect with her at alexispauline.com.